TO HEAL AS JESUS HEALED

Barbara Shlemon Ryan
Dennis Linn and
Matthew Linn

Resurrection Press
Mineola • New York

Imprimi Potest: Bruce F. Biever, S.J.
             Provincial

Excerpts from the English translation of the Roman Missal © 1973, Inter-
national Committee on English in the Liturgy, Inc. (ICEL); and excerpts
from the English translation of the Rite of Anointing and Pastoral Care of
the Sick © 1973, ICEL. All rights reserved.

Excerpts from The Jerusalem Bible, copyright © 1966 by Darton,
Longman & Todd, Ltd. and Doubleday & Company, Inc. Used by permis-
sion of the publisher.

Revised edition published in 1997 by
             Resurrection Press, Ltd.
             P.O. Box 248
             Williston Park, NY 11596

Second Printing — October, 1998

© 1997 by Matthew Linn, Dennis Linn and Barbara Shlemon Ryan

ISBN 1-878718-36-3

Library of Congress Catalog Card Number: 96-72289

Cover design by John Murello

Printed in the United States of America

Contents

Foreword
to the Revised Edition

Why have we revised this book? On the one hand, our ministry is much the same as when we wrote the first edition in 1978. Today the three of us are still giving healing retreats full time and praying for physical healing in many of the same ways we suggested twenty years ago. Many other people must still be praying for physical healing in these ways, too, since this book has sold over 100,000 copies in English and has been translated into several languages. All over the world we still hear the same question: "How should I pray for my sick _____ (mother, friend, dog, etc.)?"

On the other hand, our ministry has changed. When we first wrote this book, our readers were primarily charismatic Christians. Since then, our audience has widened considerably and so has interest in prayer for healing. Interest in healing prayer is now so widespread that *Time* magazine recently devoted its cover story to the evidence that prayer brings healing of body, mind and spirit.[1] A recent National Institutes of Health project collected over 250 empirical studies verifying the healing effects of prayer and other religious practices.[2]

For example, cardiologist Randolph Byrd studied the effects of healing prayer at San Francisco General Hospital. He randomly divided 393 heart patients into a control group and another group that would receive intercessory prayer over ten months. Although neither the staff nor the patients knew who was receiving prayer, the prayer recipients had significantly fewer complications. They were five times less likely to require antibiotics and three times less likely to develop pulmonary edema than the control group. None needed a tracheotomy, compared to twelve in the control group.[3] Even Dr. William Nolan, who has written a book expressing his skepticism about faith healing, said, "Maybe we doctors ought to be writing on our order sheets, 'Pray three times a day.'"[4]

Some of our revisions are intended to speak to this broader audience, without sacrificing our roots in the Charismatic Renewal. This movement gave us the gift of experiencing Jesus' personal love and his desire to heal us. We want to share this gift in a way that will speak to people from a wide variety of backgrounds.

Not only has our audience changed, but so have we. Watching over time how healing occurs has taught us that it occurs over time . . . in other words, we've learned that healing is a process. And we've learned how much God respects that process. In the first edition, we wrote things like, "You must forgive," or "You should believe." Today we are less likely to tell people where they should be and more likely to encourage them to take in God's love wherever they are. In a sense, healing for us is simpler today than it was twenty years ago. We've learned that healing happens whenever we acknowledge our pain and take in love.

A second change in us is that we have become far more sensitive to how language itself can wound people or heal them. As we reread the first edition of this book, we felt embarrassed by our exclusively masculine language for human beings and for God. In this revision we have tried to make amends.

Maybe you are asking the question we still hear all over the world, "How should I pray for my sick _____ (mother, friend, dog, etc.)?" May this book help you to heal as Jesus healed.

—Dennis & Matt
—Barbara

Introduction

Matt, Dennis and I were giving a workshop at St. Vincent Hospital in Toledo, Ohio when they first suggested I collaborate on writing a book. They showed me a preliminary outline, which greatly interested me because it involved exploring the new Roman Catholic rite for the Sacrament of the Sick.

In my first book, *Healing Prayer*,[1] I described the tremendous changes which occurred in my nursing career after observing a patient healed through sacramental anointing. The year was 1964 and the rite was then known as Extreme Unction, the "final anointing." In this case, however, it became not a preparation for death but a blessing which conferred physical healing and new life.

The new Rite of Anointing encourages the whole church to recognize healing prayer as a normal factor in our Christian lives. We are told to expect that physical healing and wholeness will result from utilizing the power of the sacrament, and we are called to deepen our faith in God's willingness to make us healthy.

Unfortunately, there remains in the minds of many a great deal of confusion surrounding the use of this sacrament. They continue to refer to it as the Last Rites, as the final anointing, to be given only as death is approaching. Some hospital patients who have not been instructed in the purpose of the new rite have become hysterical when the priest began to administer the Sacrament of the Sick, requiring sedation and hours of reassurance concerning their physical condition.

Others receive the anointing with very little faith in its ability to heal their illnesses. They view the sacrament as a nice ritual and a gesture of comfort by the Church, but they fail to appropriate the power for wholeness which it offers.

On the other hand, many Christians *are* appropriating the power for healing which they find available not only through the new rite of anointing, but also through prayers for physical healing. For example, in the summer of 1977, eight hundred priests attended a healing service in Steubenville, Ohio. Because of the powerful prayers of their fellow priests, by the end of that evening five hundred priests had stood to claim a physical healing.

As I travel around the country teaching Christians to pray for their sick, I'm discovering a tremendous desire on the part of the laity to become instruments for God's healing love. In Light of Christ Catholic Church, Clearwater, Florida, a brief announcement was read one Sunday morning, inviting people to volunteer for an intercessory telephone prayer-chain. Without any further explanation, eighty-eight individuals signed up to pray for others, especially for the physical healing of the sick. Such a response indicates a desire to answer some of the more common questions about healing prayer, such as: What is God's will concerning suffering? Who has the gifts to minister to the sick?

It is my hope that this book will dispel some of the confusion surrounding both the official Rite of Anointing and unofficial prayers for physical healing, thereby encouraging more of the faithful to receive the wholeness available through these methods. They are tremendous sources of grace and life, freely given to us by a heavenly Father who loves us more deeply than we can ask for or imagine.

—*Barbara*

Prologue
The Struggle to Pray for Physical Healing

I learned the hard way about stepping forward to pray with others for physical healing. Several years ago I gave a thirty-day retreat to Carol, whose deafness made it necessary for her to lip-read. For thirty days we met for one hour each day. During this time I felt that, if I were to pray with her about her deafness, her hearing could be restored. But what if I prayed with Carol and her hearing wasn't restored? Her faith might be weakened, making it difficult during the retreat for Carol to trust God, let alone to trust her retreat director.

Day after day, as I directed Carol, I entertained many thoughts of praying with her for a restoration of her hearing. At times I would consider how miracles happened only in the early Church, when atheists needed the witness value of miracles. As those thoughts drifted by, I would thank God that our generation was beyond needing miracles of physical healing. I rationalized about how fortunate Carol and I were because her deafness could call both of us to greater faith.

Yet, on other days, I could convince myself that maybe God would heal small things like my upset stomach, but probably nothing as big as deafness. I remembered a few times when I did pray about "big" things such as cancer and not much change had taken place. In one instance, the person was inconsiderate enough to die on me—and I wasn't prepared to experience another "failure."

Because I feared failing and had lost confidence in Jesus working through my prayers, I started thinking of ways in which Carol might be healed. I could concede that Jesus might heal Carol's condition only if she went to a special place such as Lourdes or Fatima, or only if she had someone special like Kathryn Kuhlman pray with her. My twelve years of intellectual seminary training came in handy as I imagined ways that Jesus might heal Carol, ways which would not involve me.

For thirty days I struggled, trying to involve myself in facing Carol's deafness with her. In the end, my fears won out. I failed to discuss her condition, avoided praying with her about it, and she left the retreat as physically deaf as she came in.

Even though I had given up, Carol had not. A year later I received a letter from her telling me: "I can hear dripping water, people behind me, birds, wind. . . . it is all like music." She had asked some friends to pray over her and her hearing was totally restored! Jesus ignored all my tip-toeing around; he healed Carol without demanding that she find Kathryn Kuhlman or journey to Lourdes. Carol's physicians confirmed that her hearing was normal, despite the fact that she still has the same physical damage (genetic neural defect with auditory nerve damage). Carol continues to hear normally—even while carrying on phone conversations with her chicken-hearted retreat director.

When I heard that a group of friends had prayed and Jesus had restored Carol's hearing, I felt both delighted and sad. I felt delighted that Carol could hear, but saddened that I hadn't stepped out to pray with her. I also felt saddened when I remembered the other people I had passed by and left to suffer, simply because I had neglected to pray for physical healing with them.

That sadness helped me to say "yes." "Yes, I will try to face problems with people like Carol and, when appropriate, offer to pray for physical healing." I was willing to begin putting to death my desire to be in control of every situation, and to allow Jesus to act his most loving way through me.

After I said "yes" to praying for physical healing, I was still left with the question of how to pray with someone like Carol. How do you pray for physical healing when, first of all, a person is willing to be prayed with and, second, when you sense that the time is right and you should be the one to do the praying?

In trying to discover healthy ways in which the Spirit might lead us to pray, Matt and I found ourselves drawn to ask Christians from many denominations to pray with us. No longer is healing prayer limited to the Pentecostal or Assembly of God Churches. Episcopalians (especially since the 1908 Lambeth Conference) and Roman Catholics (especially since the new Rite of Anointing in 1974), anoint their sick with oil and expect physical healing.

I received one of my greatest surprises in the use of anointing with oil when Matt and I attended a weekly healing service in an Episcopalian Church. This anointing service, filled with people on a Wednesday morning, celebrated two things. First, the physical healings that had occurred since last week's service and, second, the physical healings that they were currently seeking.

Since that Wednesday morning, we have witnessed the healing power of God in many Christian churches. Even in the few nonsacramental churches where there is no anointing with oil, much of their prayer for physical healing is based on traditional anointing rites, or on the same scriptural foundation.

Each of the following chapters will deal with one of the twelve sections of the new Roman Catholic ritual for anointing the sick. This Roman ritual is found on pages 95ff. of this book. We use the Roman ritual because it has evolved through twenty centuries, thus revealing the history of healing prayer, and because it includes prayers similar to those used by other Christian denominations. We hope that this view of the Rite and its history of healing prayer will enable individuals of all faiths to express better their own unique healing prayer.[1]

Since healing prayer is not limited to Roman Catholic

priests ministering the Sacrament of Anointing, we will also explore what others, like Barbara who prays fruitfully for healing, have learned about healing prayer. They can assist all of us to pray each part of the Rite so the sick will receive all the Lord's healing love; whether in the brief Rite of Anointing itself, or in its extension through healing prayer in the days that follow.

*—**Dennis***

Chapter 1
Introductory Rite

During Carol's retreat, I directed her through the *Spiritual Exercises* of St. Ignatius. For thirty days I prayed and fasted, prayed and fasted; and for thirty days Carol prayed and fasted, prayed and fasted. The purpose of the retreat was to help Carol to know Jesus intimately so she would be willing to lay down everything for him. Though the experience of the retreat gave Carol the desire to do this, the experience of Jesus healing her deafness gave Carol an even greater desire to lay down everything for him.

Four hundred years ago when St. Francis Xavier wished to give non-Christian orientals a sense of intimacy with Jesus, he didn't start with a 30-day retreat. He trained the children in the village to pray for healing.[1] After training the children, Xavier would send them off to the villages to pray for their parents, relatives and friends. Those who were healed would then seek Xavier to find out how they could know the Healer more intimately, and many would eventually lay down everything to follow Jesus.

The introductory rite of the Roman ritual for anointing the sick declares what I discovered with Carol, and what Francis Xavier discovered with the children of India: Jesus answers the prayers of lay people when they pray for physical healing. Praying for physical healing is not limited to saints like Francis Xavier or to "professional people" such as faith healers and ministers. Rather, praying for physical healing is for ordinary people, lay people, friends or relatives, adults or children, or even one of the coastal fishermen, a corner prostitute or a tax collector whom Jesus asked to come follow him by healing in his name.

In recognizing that praying for physical healing also belongs to lay people, the new Roman Rite for Anointing made two major changes: 1) Ideally, anointing is to be a *communal* rite utilizing not only the priest's but also the lay people's prayer power for healing. 2) Anointing is a rite for *healing* the sick rather than preparing the dying for death. Though the introductory rite includes only two parts, each part indicates one of those changes. In the first part, the greeting, the priest encourages all the lay people—including doctors, nurses, family, relatives and friends—to join their prayer power to heal. In the second part, the priest explains the Rite with a reading from James which indicates that the Rite's focus is not preparation for death but, rather, preparation for physical healing.

The old Rite stressed the priest's prayer for a happy death and not the lay people's prayer for healing. Remember the days when the priest came to anoint a sick relative? The priest came in the door, disappeared into the sick person's bedroom and left without saying a word. In the new Rite, the priest returns to early Christian tradition and invites the lay people to pray too. The reading from James (5:13–16) states that when anyone is sick, the elders should pray over that person. Though the "elders" who prayed with the sick may have at first been Christians designated by the community, within a few years not just elders but all family members were designated to pray for their sick. Centuries later, when a bishop questioned the current practice of lay anointing, Pope Innocent I (418 A.D.) declared that consecrated oil was to be used for healing by all Christians for "the needs of the members of their household."[2]

Unlike Baptism, Eucharist and Confession, during the first four hundred years little attention was paid to the Rite of Anointing because all Christians, not just a priest, were generally involved. Frequently the oil was blessed at the Eucharist, then sent home and kept in the medicine cabinet. St. John Chrysostom couldn't keep oil in his sanctuary lamp because the people considered it blessed oil and kept taking it home to anoint their sick. This lay anointing continued through the eighth century, began to die off, but never totally died off until 1758. For example, the Council of Trent (c. 1550 A.D.) gave ecclesial approval to the lay anointing practiced in France and Italy. But approval stopped in 1758 when the Thomas Netter seminary textbook stated that previous textbook editions had erred in allowing laity to anoint the sick.[3]

Just as lay people are once again becoming ministers of

the Eucharist, they may also again become ministers of the Sacrament of the Sick.[4] Though the priest presently administers the sacrament, lay people are once again given a central role as the priest encourages them to join in celebrating the Rite. All celebrating the Rite should "offer the sick love and help"[5] and should "pray with the sick"[6] both "before and after the celebration of the sacrament."[7] Because it is both prayer and their caring, loving presence which makes Jesus' healing love tangible in this sacrament, those celebrating should approach "in a friendly manner."[8] The sacrament publicly celebrates and brings to the sick the loving, praying community of the Church that is present not just in the patient's room but in all parts of the world.

Anointing, like all other sacraments, publicly celebrates in a few moments what the Church expects us as Christians to do every moment of our lives. Thus a sacrament such as reconciliation focuses on receiving forgiveness while a sacrament such as matrimony focuses on giving of ourself completely to another person. But both the forgiveness and the giving of ourself completely to another need to be lived out in every moment of our life. The sacrament of anointing ought to be lived out daily, not only by caring for the sick with a back rub or a phone call, but also by "praying with the sick" both "before and after the celebration of the sacrament."

Besides focusing on the role of the lay people, the new Rite also varies from the old Rite by emphasizing the healing of sickness rather than preparing the dying for death. The old rite was only given to people on their deathbed, and was even given to people who had already died. The

U.S. Bishops' Conference made it clear that the new Rite of Anointing is for the sick and that "the revised rite has removed the danger of death as a condition for the reception of the sacrament."[9] Since the new rite is about healing the sick, it is for those who are seriously ill, and "there is no reason for scruples" in judging who is seriously ill.[10] For example, the new rite is recommended especially for older people in a weakened condition, although no dangerous illness is present.

The new rite's concern for physical healing is evident in the reading from James 5:14–15, which explains:

> Is there anyone sick among you? Let [that person] call for the elders of the church, and let them pray over him [or her] and anoint him [or her] in the name of the Lord. This prayer, made in faith, will save the sick [person]. The Lord will *restore* his [or her] health, and if he [or she] has committed any sins, they will be forgiven.

The writer of James states that the prayers for healing will *restore* the sick person. "Restore" (*egerein*), when used in New Testament times, refers to physical healing (e.g., Mt 9:5–7; Mk 1:31; Acts 3:7), even bringing back to life one who had died. Physical healing was foremost in the thoughts of the early Christians when they prayed for the sick with blessings based on James. All thirteen blessings of oil still in existence from that period mention physical healing. The five most ancient blessings for the sick mention only physical healing and do not explicitly refer to spiritual effects. The Greek Church has retained this focus through the centuries and, even today, emphasizes physical healing through anointing with oil.

Only after the eighth century was anointing with oil used mainly for the dying rather than as a means for physical healing of the sick. Why this gradual shift from the lay people praying with the sick for physical healing, to the priests praying with the dying for a happy death? Among the many reasons are, first, a desire for redemptive suffering rather than for healing; second, a delay in the anointing until deathbed confession and, third, lay abuses of oil.

First, Christians prayed less for physical healing and more for redemptive suffering when the age of martyrdom ceased. Unfortunately for healing, Emperor Constantine (c. 300 A.D.) made Christianity the official religion of the Roman Empire, thus stopping the flow of martyrs' blood. Since they could no longer die for Jesus, Christians gave their bodies to Jesus when suffering illness. There soon developed a theology of illness as redemptive suffering, ignoring prayer for healing of illness.

Second, after the fifth century, confession of sins gradually became a requirement when priests ministered the sacrament of anointing. Since the church imposed extreme confessional penances (e.g. to spend years fasting or in a monastery), most people put off confession and anointing by a priest until they had dug their graves. Even after penances were relaxed and confession became more frequent, people still clung to the old practice of waiting until death to be anointed by a priest.

Third, because of abuses, by the ninth century lay people lost most privileges of anointing with oil. As martyrs became more rare, veneration for them increased, and Christians felt unworthy to pray for healing unless at a martyr's shrine or using martyr's relics. Soon the selling of spiritual favors and oil at these shrines grew into a profitable business, attracting greedy merchants or leading to superstitious practices. In an effort to stop these abuses, the use of oil was more and more restricted to the clergy, especially through the eighth century Carolingian reform. Furthermore, the prayers for anointing the sick were inserted unfortunately in many Carolingian rituals right after deathbed penance, thus, again, linking anointing with praying for the dying.

But today in the new Rite, since anointing is no longer associated with praying for the dying, we are again invited to join the priest in using our prayer power for physical healing. In praying for physical healing, we are responding to the promise Jesus extended to us, "they will lay their hands on the sick, who will recover" (Mark 16:18).

Unfortunately, we sometimes believe, as St. Augustine did, that only first-century Christianity needed the witness value of physical healing. But two years after Augustine drew this conclusion, he had witnessed seventy healings in his own church, and this forced him to retract his previous statement and to proclaim that healing was indeed meant for his own fourth century Christians. In inviting all to pray for physical healing, the introductory rite declares with Augustine that healing is for all Christians, whether they belong to the fourth or twenty-first century, just as it was for Christians of the first century.

—Dennis

For more than a dozen years the Lord has been teaching me about my responsibility as a lay person to pray for the sick. My book, *Healing Prayer* describes my first feeble attempts in exercising the commission Jesus gave to "whoever believes in me." There is little room for excusing ourselves when we take John 14:12 literally, and accept the fact that we are called to do the same works as Jesus. "I tell you most solemnly, whoever believes in me will perform the same works as I do myself, [that person] will perform even greater works, because I am going to the Father." Throughout the Acts of the Apostles we encounter early Christians continuing to heal the sick, as Jesus did, especially those who were lame and paralyzed. My experience has shown me that these "acts" are supposed to continue in today's church through the hands and hearts of those who are willing to pray for the sick.

Many lay people attend religious services, but seldom realize their role in bringing healing to others because they consider themselves inadequate, unworthy, unspiritual or too sinful to ever be an instrument of God. One wonders what would happen if all who call themselves Christian decided to exercise their spiritual gifts on a given Sunday morning. The power of atomic energy would pale in comparison!

I often hear from Christians who have found themselves in situations where they prayed with another, out of sheer desperation, only to discover God answering in very profound ways. One such incident involved a delivery room nurse who assisted at the birth of a one-and-one-half-pound premature stillborn baby boy. The infant was placed in a bassinet while the nurses finished caring for the mother and returning her to the ward. Nearly ten minutes had passed since the delivery, but the R.N., who had never prayed over anyone, began to feel that she should lay hands on the baby and ask Jesus to give him life. It seemed so ridiculous, since the doctor had already signed the death certificate, and the infant had been without oxygen for so long, but there was no one else who could intercede at that moment.

The nurse placed her hands on the tiny baby and asked Jesus to bless his lifeless form. Within seconds he began to breathe, moving his arms and legs. She quickly took him into the nursery where he was placed in an isolette and continued to make remarkable progress. After a year's time, the child appears to be developing normally, and the nurse is still awed at this amazing response to prayer.

A good place to begin exercising the ability to pray with one another is in our own homes. Family members are natural channels of healing for one another. Parents can do themselves, and their children, a great favor if they pray for them on a regular basis, asking God's blessing on their households. Parents are natural instruments of healing for their children, even if they have never attended a workshop on the subject. It seems only logical that the Creator who entrusted us with the responsibility of rearing youngsters, would also aid us in the process when we invoke God's help.

Scripture relates the story of a synagogue chief, Jairus,

who begs Jesus to come to his home because his 12-year-
old daughter lay dying (Lk 8:40–56). By the time they
arrived at the home, the mourners were wailing over the
girl's body. Therefore, Jesus sent everyone away except
Peter, James, John and the *girl's parents*. Undoubtedly they
were a healthy influence because the girl returned to life
and Jesus told them to give her something to eat. Perhaps
Jairus and his wife will inspire parents to become instruments for their children's wholeness.

My friends, Kathy and Tom O'Regan of Highland Park,
Illinois, are a beautiful example of a couple who understand this principle. Their young son, Joey, was born with
multiple birth defects, i.e., cleft palate, cleft lip, hip defor-
mities, heart murmur. From the moment of his birth, Joey's
parents surrounded him with loving prayer; the kind of
intercession Francis MacNutt describes as "soaking
prayer."[11] As a result, one hip has spontaneously healed, he
has shown remarkable recuperative ability through his various surgeries, and maintains a joyful disposition which
draws people to him. Kathy and Tom discovered increased
love for each other as they joined together to minister to
their little son.

Children can also be wonderful channels of healing
love for their parents, as witnessed by the following illustra-
tion sent to me by Thea Connally of Palatine, Illinois.

"I had been sick for eighteen years, having spent
four months in the National Institute of Health,
blind, crippled and with a rare skin disease. I had
been in a wheel chair on and off, blind, on and off,

had stomach ulcers, kidney infections, rheumatoid arthritis in every joint of my body. My eyes hemorrhaged and I developed cysts and boils within and without my body. The last three years of having these diseases, my venal system was being destroyed and I would get blood clots in both legs. I coughed up blood now and then, and was severely anemic. I was told that my bone marrow was not producing sufficient amounts of new blood cells to keep me alive. I would need transfusions because any form of iron, taken orally, was radically destroying my stomach with ulcers. I was allergic to everything but sleep.

"My four children were becoming belligerent, rebellious and cynical. It was necessary for them to do so much that there wasn't much time or joy for them. I tried desperately to hide my feelings, but despair, guilt and frustration would burst forth on the children in one form or another.

"One day my 14-year-old son came home from some meeting and said that he'd been baptized in the Holy Spirit. With that statement I thought a heart attack or stroke would be added to my already numerous diseases. I said, 'Our church preaches only one baptism. What have you done?' He very patiently and lovingly showed me in scripture where this baptism of the Holy Spirit is. He convinced me that he was not going to hell for this. Week by week I saw him change as he consistently reacted with love and obedience. He spoke of a real living Jesus who was changing his life. I felt like an ogre in the light of his love.

"One day, after hearing more bad news regarding

some of my tests, I was in the living room crying for three hours. I didn't know how to prepare my children for living without me. I had two sons, 14 and 9, and two daughters, 12 and 3. My 14-year-old son came home from school and saw me crying. He knew what I was going through. He held my arm and as he prayed aloud for me, I felt a strange, awesome sensation, I stopped crying and felt at peace. Something good but unexplainable was happening to me."

This young boy's prayer on behalf of his mother enabled her to begin attending prayer meetings where she received further ministering until, after a year's time, she was pronounced totally healed by her doctors. Every laboratory test was normal and Thea was able to assume a normal, productive life. She and her husband, Ralph, have gone on to develop their own ministry to the sick. All this proceeded from the effects of a youngster's petition for his mother.

The greeting in the new rite invites all people to use the healing power of Jesus in praying for the needs of others.

May we each accept that invitation.

—***Barbara***

Chapter 2
Penitential Rite

After the introduction, the Rite of the Sick provides an opportunity to ask for forgiveness. Since the prayers ask God to forgive *us*—not just *me,* we are invited not only to receive God's forgiveness but also to extend his complete forgiveness toward all. Likewise to the degree that those praying for the sick can forgive one another, their prayer has more love power (Mk 11:25). Lack of forgiveness toward others and toward God seems to make it more difficult to receive healing. What we do to the least of our brothers and sisters, we do to Jesus. When we resent another, it is more difficult to receive the love of Jesus present in that person. To aid reconciliation many priests, before starting the penitential rite, pause to let the sick person recall who has hurt her the most and, thus, most needs her forgiveness.

Throughout history, Christians have recognized how helpful forgiveness is as a preparation for healing. Jesus prepared the paralytic to walk by first forgiving his deeper sinful paralysis (Mk 2:1–12). James 5:15–16 stressed that the sick person's sins would be forgiven. St. Bede (735 A.D.) cited both James' epistle and Innocent I's decree that penitents should not be anointed for healing until they were forgiven.

As mentioned in the previous chapter, with the passage of time, more stress was placed on confessing sins to a priest until anointing finally became associated with death-bed confession. However, the new Rite recommends sacramental confession as a means of healing and recommends that "whenever it is necessary, the priest should hear the sacramental confession of the sick person, if possible, before the celebration of anointing."[1] Sacramental confession would be particularly healing for those experiencing heavy guilt or a deep awareness of having harmed the Christian community.[2]

In situations where sacramental confession is not used, the penitential rite is prayed in order that we can give and receive forgiveness with one another. St. Bede suggests, along with James, that even those praying for the sick are to confess their daily sins to one another, enabling them to become better channels for Jesus' healing love. When we give a workshop on healing, we find the best preparation is to share our hearts, especially any misunderstandings which may have hurt one another. When we do that, we clear the channels for healing to happen through us.

Not only Christian tradition but also modern medicine

teaches the power of healing through forgiveness. Since Dr. Walter Cannon, in 1914, measured the physiological changes in a cat experiencing anger and fear stimulated by a barking dog, researchers have probed the body's "fight-flight" response triggered by fear, anger or the self-anger of guilt.[3] A person who has migraines will probably have his headaches recur unless, through forgiveness, he deals with the hurts outside himself that create anger, and the hurts within himself that create guilt. The heart patient must also deal with the free-floating anger of her "type-A behavior" that pressures her to do more in less time.[4] Anger and guilt also play a role in triggering or aggravating neurodermatitis, hypertension, asthma, colitis, rheumatoid arthritis and a host of other illnesses. We also know that a body free from excessive anger, fear and guilt heals faster and is more immune to illness.[5]

The Lord's Prayer "forgive us our trespasses as we forgive those who trespass against us" illuminates Jesus' way to heal the fear, anger and guilt that are the breeding grounds for most physical illness. Fear underlies anger and guilt. We get angry when what we fear is outside ourselves, and guilty when that we fear is within ourselves. The first way to resolve anger and guilt is to change the things we need to change. But secondly, we need to forgive. When we forgive another, we heal the hurt underneath our anger. When we forgive ourselves, we heal the hurt underneath our guilt.

Unloving behavior, with its accompanying feelings of anger and guilt, often but not always, becomes a factor in illness. Jesus pointed out that neither the blind man nor his parents had sinned (Jn 9:3). Often the sin belongs to others: the greedy polluting factories belching out cancerous fumes, the inadequate wages and health care we offer the poor, our lack of care and prayer for the sick, our inability to help another before his burdens lead to physical or emotional illness.

As Dr. Hans Selye showed, stress is a factor in nearly every illness, and we make one another ill to the degree that we create stress in our environment or fail to relieve it.[6] Maybe that's why James (5:14–16) suggests that those who pray for the sick confess their sins to one another, enabling them to pray the heartfelt prayer of a "good" person, one who creates more goodness.

While living with the Sioux Indians, who were under constant stress from their poverty and disintegrating culture, we came to appreciate the importance of dealing with stress in order to assure continued healing. We noticed how many Sioux were healed of arthritis and ulcers through prayer while attending conferences away from the sufferings of the reservation, only to have the symptoms recur following the return to their stressful environment, where there is about 70% unemployment and rampant alcoholism.

However, if they found jobs, if their spouses quit drinking, or if their marriages were reconciled, they could be prayed with and, this time, remain free from rheumatoid arthritis or ulcers. For healing prayer to be more effective, we must all confess our failure to make the love of Jesus more present in our environment and, with his help, change what can be changed. We give the daily bread of health when we can say: "forgive us our trespasses as we forgive those who trespass against us."

—Matt and Dennis

The first step in praying for healing always involves forgiveness. Perhaps that is why not only the Rite of Anointing but even the celebration of the Eucharist begin with forgiveness. There does not seem to be any greater deterrent to wholeness than a lack of forgiveness in our lives and, no matter how we try to justify our position, it remains an unavoidable obstacle.

We have encountered numerous persons who experienced healing after they forgave others, God or themselves. In March, 1976, Matt, Dennis and I prayed with a Canadian priest with a diagnosed slipped disc, which made it difficult for him to walk and impossible for him to bend over. This condition persisted for two years until. . . .

> "Last night I sat there, and it was a humiliation to sit in front of all of you. I was asked to pull my shirt up (so doctors could check his spine), and that was the ultimate. I said to Jesus, 'Here I am making a fool of myself, but I believe.' So they began to pray and pray and nothing happened to me except a great peace. Then someone said, 'John, forgive and fill your heart with forgiveness.' I really felt that I had forgiven everyone, but I began going over, one-by-one, the people who had hurt

me, forgave them again and, immediately, things
began to happen.

"There was a hand touching me right at the bot-
tom of my back, and immediately electricity
passed from that hand and began soaking into my
spine. It hurt a little bit, like when you have surgery for a cyst, which I had just undergone. You
don't feel the pain because of the anesthesia, but
you feel the pulling—and there was pulling going
on in my back. That curve is not there any more.
Walking, I felt very clumsy on my feet—now I am
more steady. I keep saying: 'Lord, you are tremendous!' I really want to thank all who prayed for me
because I really felt the body of Christ there, and
I felt your love and compassion which was very
strong. Jesus was as real there as he was in Gali-
lee, and he touched me through you."

John's healed spine was immediately confirmed by several doctors who had helped us with the prayer. Two years
later, John is still totally healed. Forgiveness seems to be one
of the most common ways to open ourselves to Jesus' healing power.

Sometimes forgiveness seems nearly impossible
because we associate forgiveness with a "feeling" of love
toward another. Though this may happen as forgiveness
deepens, forgiveness usually begins by deciding to cease
harboring anger towards another or guilt towards ourself.
This act of our will opens the door of our spirit to enable
God to begin to bless our lives. Healing often occurs when
we begin exercising this discipline of forgiveness.

Though it may be easy to understand the need of forgiving ourself or another person, many Christians have difficulty understanding why it might be necessary, or even possible, to forgive the One who created us. Of course God is sinless, and we are not denying the perfection of God's will for us. What we are recognizing is our own imperfection in perceiving this love and the times we have misinterpreted God's actions. Perhaps the following excerpt from a letter written to me by Margaret Cossentino, a registered nurse, will illustrate this point:

> "When I arrived at the retreat on Friday evening, I was in quite a bit of pain. Two weeks before the weekend I had a miscarriage at three months and developed phlebitis in my left leg. During the Friday night session in the Chapel, I was able to 'forgive God' for this miscarriage, allowing his healing love to replace the anger and resentment I felt. What a tremendous relief it was for me! Early Saturday morning, about 3:30 a.m., I awoke with the feeling I should be praying. Soon I realized I was sitting Indian-style on the bed and was comfortable. I got up and walked on my leg which was no longer painful. In fact, I jumped up and down to see if it would hurt and it didn't. I should have told you about it then, but I was a little skeptical as to how long it would last since this was my second bout with phlebitis. Now it has been seven months and I have not had a twinge of discomfort in my leg."

Sometimes the person we need to forgive is not God or

another person, but rather ourselves. The penitential rite offers an opportunity to confess our faults and receive absolution.

"Happy the [person] whom Yahweh accuses of no guilt,
    whose spirit is incapable of deceit!
All the time I kept silent, my bones were wasting away with
    groans, day in, day out;
day and night your hand lay heavy on me;
my heart grew parched as stubble in summer drought.
At last I admitted to you I had sinned; no longer concealing
    my guilt,
I said, 'I will go to Yahweh and confess my fault'.
And you, you have forgiven the wrong I did, have pardoned
    my sin."

                                              (Psalm 32:1b-5)

I recall praying with a young woman who had suffered from constant migraine headaches for several years. The onset of the condition occurred immediately after she had undergone a medical abortion for a three-month pregnancy. She convinced herself that the abortion was justified, even bragged about the operation, but her body was contradicting the rationale. She finally went to confession and her migraines completely disappeared. She later told me that it wasn't difficult to believe God could forgive her failing, but she had a terrific battle learning to forgive herself.

As we can see, the penitential rite in the Sacrament of the Sick is very important to the one receiving the prayer.

—*Barbara*

Chapter 3
Scripture Reading

The third section of the Rite of Anointing designates that a suitable passage from scripture be read by one of those present. This practice finds its roots not only in Jesus, who began his Galilean healing ministry by reading from Isaiah (Lk 4:18–19), but also in first-century Christian communities which used James 5:14–16 as they prayed for healing. We have chosen a passage from John's Gospel:

> I tell you most solemnly,
> whoever believes in me
> will perform the same works as I do myself,
> [that person] will perform even greater works,
> because I am going to the Father.
> Whatever you ask for in my name I will do,
> so that the Father may be glorified in the Son.

If you ask for anything in my name,
I will do it.

(Jn 14: 12–14)

Why then doesn't more happen when we ask for healing in Jesus' name? Jesus is so eager to heal that he healed
even on the Sabbath, and healed without being asked,
though he knew it meant the authorities would plot to kill
him (Mk 3:1–6; Jn 5:1–18). He was just as eager for his disciples to heal the sick and his last words recorded in Mark
are, "And these signs will accompany those who believe.
. . . they will lay their hands upon the sick and they will
recover" (Mk 16:17–18). If Jesus is so eager to heal through
us, why doesn't it happen more often in prayer?

Jesus promised: "Whatever you ask in my name, I will
do it." Prayer often seems futile, because to ask "in the
name of Jesus, heal Ann," may not really be asking in Jesus'
name. To the Jew the name signified everything about a person's character. Therefore, asking in Jesus' name would
mean asking with Jesus' thoughts and feelings, just as he
would. When we are asking for the healing he wishes, Jesus
promises to answer our prayer. The scripture reading of
Jesus' healing comes early in the Rite so we can put on the
mind and heart of Jesus to pray in his name. We should also
pray for Jesus' mind to guide us in the choice of a scripture
passage that will speak directly to the sick person's needs.

If we don't see our prayer being answered, it is sometimes because we are focusing on our way rather than praying in the name of Jesus, with his mind and heart, seeking
his way and time. Sometimes we are asking for a migraine

to be healed, and missing how Jesus first desires to heal the circumstances so the migraine won't recur.

How do we know the way in which Jesus wishes to heal? The challenge is not to have more faith in our faith, but to have enough love so we can see the more loving way Jesus wishes to heal. We come before Jesus and silently listen to the way he is speaking of his love for his loved one. Sickness and pain are usually not Jesus' will because they leave a wake of self-centeredness, making it difficult to love God, others and ourselves. Whenever this occurs, we can be sure that Jesus wants to heal the illness or at least heal the way it chokes our power to love.

Some people have a rare vocation to suffer redemptively and to grow in their power to love as they endure their illness. When working as an orderly, Matt cared for a saintly Dominican, Paschal Kelly, who suffered for twenty years from multiple sclerosis, despite prayer for healing. He would lie in bed, not able to turn his head or scratch a maddening itch.

Despite the fact that Paschal was confined to a hospital, Matt relates that "many people from all over the world—including Hollywood stars—came to see him. What they came to witness was how Paschal's suffering made him like Jesus. I would put him into a wheelchair and take him to visit the sickest, most depressed patient. It was difficult for any patient to feel sorry for himself after seeing Paschal, smiling from his wheelchair."

What Matt witnessed was Paschal's ability to reach the poor, the lonely and those who felt abandoned, because he experienced utter dependence on God's love. This type of

suffering is redemptive to the degree that it leads us to give
and receive Jesus' love. Suffering is redemptive if it is
healing.

Finally, some people are to become like Jesus, not
through the ordinary way of healing or the rarer way of
redemptive suffering, but through the ultimate healing,
death, with its gift of a resurrected and healed body. There
is a time to pray, not for healing, but for relief of pain and
a happy death.

How do we know when to pray for a person to die?
Usually, we wouldn't pray for death if a person is depressed
or desiring death because she is tortured by pain or a problem. We would first pray for relief of the pain, problem or
depression, so that a person can choose death, not because
she is running from something painful, but because she is
running toward God. If a dying person is choosing God
rather than running from life, then we are often led to pray
for a happy death.

Whether we are praying for death or for life, our prayer
becomes more powerful as we become a channel of Jesus'
love. People in love don't just say "I love you," they day-
dream about each other. Deep love is deeper than con-
scious words and flows into the imagination to influence
the subconscious. Healing prayer, too, should utilize the
imagination to remove the subconscious blocks to Jesus'
healing love.[1] Picturing the person whole, lets Jesus give his
healing love through our subconscious imagination, and
deepens our own trust in his love. This also helps the sick
person. The patient who imagines himself getting well generally heals faster.

Dr. Carl Simonton, a leading oncologist, finds that hopeless cases of cancer often go into remission once the patient can imagine and believe his phagocytes are like fish eating the cancer cells and bringing health.[2] Every basketball player knows how to make more baskets by imagining the free throw splitting the net rather than bouncing off the rim. Praying in Jesus' name means removing subconscious barriers by imagining the healing already taking place.

For a long time we avoided imagining and describing the healing we thought Jesus wanted for fear of raising false hopes. Now we simply let the sick person know that the way we imagine healing may fall short of God's perfect plan, which is infinitely beyond what we can ask for or imagine (Eph 3:20). Listening to the scriptures thus leads us all to pray in Jesus' name—as he would. Thus, our prayer becomes more healing as we pray more the prayer that Jesus is praying within us.

—Matt and Dennis

Scripture reading is an integral part of every sacrament, reminding us that the Bible continues to be the "living word of God." Roman Catholics are increasingly becoming more familiar with scripture as Bible study groups are now regularly scheduled in many local parishes.

The Gospel narratives give a graphic picture of Jesus' approach to sickness, since the majority of his public life was devoted to healing. Jesus had overwhelming compassion for those who were suffering, and was constantly reaching out to bring wholeness.

A sick person can receive much comfort from reading the Bible, and often discovers renewed faith as the "living word" touches the spirit. I have heard countless testimonies from people whose illness began to disappear as they invoked the power of a scripture passage.

Many times I've encouraged a person to image a particular Gospel episode and "see" Jesus ministering his healing love in today's situation. God's attitude toward sickness is the same as it was two thousand years ago, and the same touch of love is possible when we call upon the mercy of Jesus.

If someone is incapacitated and unable to read the Bible, we can perform a great service by offering to read uplifting passages of scripture. This is an apostolate which those who minister to the sick can provide.

A person in a coma is often able to hear what is being said, even if unable to respond in a visible way. This is why it is so important that only positive, affirming words are spoken at the bedside of an unconscious patient, giving messages of life and hope.

People who have survived comatose states will often be able to relate entire conversations which went on in their rooms while they were seemingly unaware. Many times such persons have related to me the tremendous effect the word of God had upon them in their helpless conditions. One woman who survived a severe auto accident declared, "I was given the courage to live when I heard my sister repeatedly saying 'I can do all things through Christ who strengthens me'" (Ph 4:13 RSV).

One dramatic example of healing through scripture happened to a man who suffered a massive stroke and was pronounced in a vegetative state by his physicians. After several weeks he was moved to a nursing home where the staff was instructed to make his lifeless body as comfortable as possible. His wife visited him every day, and for hours would sit by his bedside reading the Bible to him. Within six weeks he began to show signs of improvement as his spouse continued her daily vigil and local prayer groups began to lend their support. It was a day for much celebration when he walked out of the nursing home, showing only the slightest residual effects from his former condition, and praising God.

The Rite of Anointing tells us to choose a reading suitable for the occasion in order to focus attention on the presence of Jesus in our midst.

—Barbara

Chapter 4
Litany

Lord, through this holy anointing, come and comfort __N__ with your love and mercy.
R. Lord, hear our prayer.
Free __N__ from all harm.
R. Lord, hear our prayer.
Relieve the sufferings of all the sick (here present).
R. Lord, hear our prayer.
Assist all those dedicated to the care of the sick.
R. Lord, hear our prayer.
Free __N__ from sin and all temptation.
R. Lord, hear our prayer.
Give life and health to our brother (sister) __N__,
on whom we lay our hands in your name.
R. Lord, hear our prayer.

In this section of the Rite of Anointing, we begin to pray as did Jesus and the early Christians. Though we do not have any Western liturgical formula for anointing until after 800 A.D., we do have litanies which early Christians may have used at the time of anointing such as "bless all who live here" or "bless this dwelling." The early Christians didn't have books with printed responses to prayers, so they used a litany form of short requests, each followed by a set response such as "Lord, hear our prayer," or "Lord, have mercy." The sick, who didn't have the strength or the attention to say long prayers, could pray the litany by simply responding "Lord, hear our prayer" to whatever prayer the healthy and creative leader composed. The current litany in the Anointing of the Sick, again, gives the sick a chance to pray for themselves, for others who are sick, and especially for those "who care for the sick."

The heartfelt prayer of the sick has great power to help others. When working as a hospital chaplain, Matt would ask someone suffering great pain from surgery to pray for another near death. Very often the dying person would take a sudden turn toward recovery, or else request that Matt come to help prepare him for death.

One man, Bill, wanted nothing to do with religion until Bertha, in pain from gall bladder surgery, spent a sleepless night praying for him. About 3:00 a.m. Bill called for Matt, and he died receiving God's forgiveness and peace. Bertha also offered her pain and prayers for Mary, a 68-year-old widow barely alive and needing gall bladder surgery. Through the skills of the doctors and prayers of Bertha, Mary recovered in record time and with little pain. A patient in pain can pray with deep empathetic power for another to recover and be freed from pain.

Whether using the formal litanies or other informal prayers, the sick may themselves be healed as they intercede for others. Kathy, for example, was in fine shape, walking through the woods to our healing conference, when she dislocated her toe. An orthopedic surgeon at the conference tried, unsuccessfully, to manipulate the toe back into place. We all prayed for Kathy and felt confident that Jesus would remove the pain so she could pray and focus on the healing conference. To our surprise, nothing happened.

That night Kathy was hobbling along with a friend to get some things from her car. As she opened the car door she accidentally slammed it shut on her friend's hand. Immediately Kathy, with her throbbing foot, knew her friend's pain and prayed that Jesus might heal the hand. The pain left the hand while, at the same time, Kathy's dislocated toe popped back in place. In reaching out to heal another, Kathy was healed.[1]

During the same workshop, another lady tore a knee cartilage which locked her leg so she couldn't straighten it out. The orthopedic surgeon diagnosed this as requiring surgery. She felt moved to pray for other people who needed physical healing. Not only were many physically healed by her heartfelt prayer but, by the next morning, her own knee was healed. Now in our workshops those with similar ailments often pray with one another, since they really understand each other's suffering. They often receive healing while in prayer for a fellow sufferer. As promised long ago in Isaiah 58:6–8, when reaching out to help another, "your wound shall quickly be healed."

—Matt and Dennis

The litany in the Rite of Anointing invites everyone, including the sick person, to join in prayer, becoming actively involved in the sacrament. The one who is ill can petition God's mercy for healing of body, mind and spirit. The sick can intercede for loved ones and the medical staff. This provides a marvelous opportunity to receive Jesus' blessings. Countless people have been healed through this unselfish love "because the amount you measure out is the amount you will be given back" (Lk 6:38). As the patient reaches out in loving concern to pray for the needs of others, Jesus reaches in to answer the sick person's own desires.

I think it is especially appropriate that the sick person intercedes for the doctors, hospital staff, family and friends. The person who is ill brings great blessings by praying for those who care for her physical needs, asking that their hands become the healing hands of Jesus. Prayer can be offered for the gift of wisdom to be given to physicians so they properly diagnose and treat the illness. There are hundreds of people behind the scenes in every hospital (in laboratories, kitchens, maintenance, laundry) who would also appreciate being blessed through a patient's prayers. The litany affords an opportunity to do that very thing.

The healing love of Jesus can be more fully experienced when people unite in prayer for the one who is sick. As we join hearts in harmony with other believers, we discover the truth of the words of Jesus: "If two of you on earth agree to ask anything at all, it will be granted to you by my Father in heaven" (Mt 18:19). We sometimes discover rapid answers to our prayers when we submit the requests to fellow Christians and stop trying to carry the full weight of intercession. The phenomenal rise in the number of prayer groups throughout the world, even Protestant and Catholics praying together in war-torn Northern Ireland, gives witness to the fact that people have a deep longing to share prayer with each other.

Recently I was asked to pray with a woman hospitalized in the terminal stages of cancer. She was in constant pain with the prospect of death creating a tremendous anxiety. Several of her relatives were present in the hospital room, so I invited them to speak to Jesus concerning Betty's need for wholeness. They were somewhat self-conscious, but one, then another, began to ask Jesus to touch their beloved relative. Their discomfort quickly turned to serenity as the presence of Jesus descended upon the entire gathering. Betty's physical pain completely subsided and, within a few days, she died peacefully in her sleep.

Her sister phoned to thank me for giving the family an opportunity to pray. "We were all praying for Betty individually," she said, "but none of us had realized the importance of praying together *with* her. The experience has deepened our relationship with God and with one another."

—Barbara

Chapter 5
Laying On of Hands

The laying on of hands is a rite of healing touch practiced by the earliest Christians as they prayed over the sick (Jas 5:14). Jesus frequently used touch to heal and told his followers that "they will lay hands upon the sick, who will recover" (Mk 16:18). Thus Paul was healed of blindness as Ananias laid hands on him (Acts 9:17). To the Jew, touch bestowed one's power just as Moses laid his hand and power on Joshua (Nm 27:18–20), or as Jesus felt power go out from him when touched by the woman with the hemorrhage (Lk 8:46). Touch remained important even to the early church, as exemplified by St. Irenaeus (150 A.D.) who reports that he and others "still heal the sick by laying hands on them and they are made whole."[1]

Touch is a natural healing gift and, like all natural gifts, Jesus can use it just as he makes a gift for preaching out of the natural gift for speaking. Dr. Dolores Kreiger, professor at New York University, has taught thousands of doctors, nurses and therapists how to lay hands lovingly on their patients and thus transmit healing energy from themselves to a sick person whose illness has placed him or her in an energy "deficit."[2] Dr. Kreiger has been able to demonstrate clinically the effectiveness of touch by measuring a significant rise in hemoglobin levels in the patients who receive this treatment.

Touch can even make the difference between death and life. During World War II, orphaned English babies often died after being institutionalized, with the exception of one orphanage where a night worker lovingly held the lonely babies after finishing her cleaning tasks. Now, in every maternity ward, nurses routinely give babies one of the most powerful forms of medicine, a loving hug. Likewise, parents are encouraged to hold their babies as much as possible and mothers are encouraged to breastfeed them, not only because mother's milk is healthy, but because a mother's touch brings comfort and security. Some psychologists report that children who are not lovingly touched have a much higher incidence of schizophrenia, because they are verbally told they are loved but not tactually shown it.

Does our puritanical inhibition against touching another person also inhibit the flow of the Spirit's healing power, which was so evident in the early church? Laying on of hands should be a natural gesture communicating the care, gentleness and strength of Jesus sending his Spirit to heal. Likewise, allowing another to touch you is a natural gesture showing openness and acceptance. Laying on of hands is such an ancient and powerful gesture that every sacrament but matrimony utilizes it to confer the Holy Spirit's power.[3]

In the Rite of Anointing, hands are *silently* laid upon the sick because we are not praying our own individual healing prayer; rather, our hands have become the hands of Jesus and his church, praying in the Spirit for healing. When praying over another, we try to imagine how Jesus would lovingly touch this person. Then, in silence, we let Jesus' love in our heart flow through our hands. It's like the image of the roadside crucifix in France which was missing Jesus' hands due to the bombing of World War II. Someone who understood the laying on of hands wrote on the cross, "I have no hands but yours."

—Matt and Dennis

The importance of touch has been given quite a lot of publicity in recent years. In my area of the country you often see the bumper sticker, "Have you hugged your kid today?"—courtesy of the local mental health society. I suggest they amend the question to read, "Have you hugged *anyone* today?", since we all need these outward signs of affection, no matter how old we are.

The laying on of hands provides us with an occasion to demonstrate concern for another person as we reach out to make a physical connection, just as the sign of peace at

Mass is a time for affirming community through touch. Our hands communicate volumes of non-verbal information as we discover when shaking hands with someone. Many business people can accurately predict a person's character through the ritual of the handshake.

The scriptures are filled with accounts of the beneficial effects of the laying on of hands as practiced by Jesus and his disciples. Besides demonstrating a loving concern, there is often a transference of power as we ask Jesus to permit our hands to be instruments of his love. Many people experience a feeling of heat, tingling of nerves or slight vibrations as they pray over another. These same phenomena are also reported by the individuals receiving prayer, which makes the theory of energy-flow a possibility. Many scientific experiments are now being conducted to prove such a force exists but, with or without the proof, the results speak for themselves.

A typical letter reads:

"I had never before been 'prayed over' with the laying on of hands until the night of my first prayer meeting. The priest leading the group asked if anyone needed physical healing, and I was experiencing severe back pain due to a fall several years ago. I sat in the chair and a few members from the group laid hands on my back and began to quietly pray. It was as if an electric current went right through my spine and all the pain subsided. What a relief to be able to move about without excruciating suffering! I knew it was Jesus who touched me that night through the hands of those beautiful people, and I will be eternally grateful."

The Rite of Anointing incorporates the laying on of hands into the ritual in order that the blessing might flow through the entire body of the sick person. We are not only concerned with the salvation of the soul but also with the restoration of the body and this gesture symbolizes that truth. Jesus healed the *total person* as he walked upon this earth and, through our loving touch, God continues to bring freedom.

—*Barbara*

Chapter 6
Blessing of Oil

Just as Jesus uses the touch of loving hands to enable us to feel his healing love, so, too, he places his power in oil which tells all our senses that he is healing the whole person. The prayer for blessing this oil not only recognizes the need to expect healing of body, mind and soul, but also encourages us to treat and pray for the whole sick person. Members of the early church believed that this prayer, which is based on the bishop's "*Emitte*" prayer recorded by Hippolytus in 197 A.D., consecrated the oil with divine power so that anyone could use it with deep expectation for healing.[1] Today the bishop consecrates the oil of the sick on Holy Thursday. Priests, too, by praying the "Blessing of Oil" prayer can consecrate oil for the sacrament of the sick. The prayer expects the sick person "to be freed from pain and illness and made well again in body, mind and soul."

Healing of illness is often a process that takes place over time. When we pray over a person who is in pain, such as those with rheumatoid arthritis, often the first sign of healing is that the pain decreases or disappears. Perhaps Jesus does this first because pain is usually nonredemptive, making it difficult for a person to focus beyond herself and reach out in love. Occasionally physical healing is total and immediate, but usually it requires time if the "mind and soul" are to be brought into wholeness also.

Larry, for example, had his arthritic arm healed immediately, but returned five times to a prayer group before his knee was free of arthritis. In sharing, he noted that, "what I appreciate more than the arthritic healing was the group of people who prayed with me every week and became my first real friends. If Jesus had healed my arthritis all at once, I may not have come back, or even if I did come back, I doubt that I would know you in the same way." Sometimes physical healing is immediate, or the natural healing process is speeded up. Sometimes the healing takes place but natural damage remains, as when Carol's hearing returned despite nerve damage. Jesus knows best when and how to heal.

We should always expect prayer for healing to begin to heal the heart's fear, anger and guilt, as it did for Larry in his arthritic loneliness. Most emotional suffering is not redemptive but, like depression, chokes our power to love and to be at one with God, others and our deeper self. This healing is deepened the more we can listen to the sick person's struggles and enter into his breaking heart with the heart of Jesus. This process of inner healing of the hurtful emotions, we describe simply in our other books, listed in Resources for Further Growth at the end of this book.

Healing through prayer heals more than the body and mind. When Jesus Christ is the focus of healing, we receive the ultimate healing, the experience of being unconditionally loved by Jesus. While working in emergency rooms we saw many people leave the hospital with healed bodies, only to return a month later on a drug overdose. At a level deeper than physical health, they had the gangrenous wound of being unloved. No pills or surgery can heal their broken spirit, but when Jesus touches their wound, they become empowered to receive and give love. Those who are most alive are not necessarily those who are physically strongest, but those who feel loved and who communicate love the most. As Jesus' unconditional love touches us, the love invites us to love him and others and thus live life more fully.

Early Christians experienced so much fullness of life and healing from the oil blessed for the sick that they began to use and sell it as a magical potion needing no accompanying prayer. This led the Church to limit the use of sacramental oil to the clergy. But today oil can again be blessed non-sacramentally to use along with healing prayer for the sick. Just as lay people are invited to use holy water as an extension of baptismal water, so too, lay people are invited to anoint with oil as an extension of the sacrament of the sick. The following quote from Francis MacNutt's book, *The Power To Heal,* (Ave Maria Press, 1977) helps to explain this tradition.

Many Catholic priests are not aware of this, but there is a blessing for oil which is for everyday healing use, and which people can then take home and use in praying for each other. There is no indication that this oil is limited to the sacrament of Anointing or to the bishop or priest (although its blessing is reserved to the bishop or priest).[3]

The prayer for the non-sacramental blessing of oil is found in the Appendix on pages 104–105.

This blessing also asks that all who are anointed be freed "from all suffering and all infirmity" and that it "may bring health in body and mind to all who use it." As in the early days of Christianity, the laity are again encouraged to use this blessed oil for all bodily ailments, whether it be a simple cut or a more serious sickness. Christians relied on spontaneous anointing prayers until 800 A.D., and Christians are once again invited to use the oil for healing with spontaneous prayers that arise from their hearts.

Unfortunately many people do not trust their spontaneous heartfelt prayer. Yet prayers said with deep compassion can be more powerful than prayers by those with a more practiced gift of healing prayer.

Dennis speaks of the many times a mother has brought a sick child to him and, as only a mother can, has hugged the child and asked Dennis to pray for healing. "But when I see that hug, I am reminded of God the Mother who will never "forget her baby at the breast or fail to cherish the child of her womb" (Is 49:15). So I often tell the mother that because she loves her child more than I do, her prayer, rather than mine, will be closer to the prayer in God the Mother's heart.

"I ask her if she would mind praying the powerful prayer God has placed in her heart while I silently pray with her, and when she is finished I will simply say whatever is in my heart.

"Far more happens when a mother prays from the intense pain and love in her heart than when I pray for her child. Not only does the child get well but the mother and child grow closer as the child hears and feels the depth of the mother's love."

The gift of healing is really the gift of love. To the degree we love as Jesus did, we will anoint and heal in his name and with his power. Blessing oil, which lay people may use in anointing the sick, should make us all aware of our particular gifts for healing those we can love uniquely.

—*Barbara*
—*Matt and Dennis*

Chapter 7
Prayer of Thanksgiving

On Thanksgiving Day both body and soul are nourished as we carve the roasted turkey and give thanks for the past year's blessings. We gather around the groaning table and try to pay attention not just to the steaming raisin dressing but also to the blessing before the meal.

During our last year's Thanksgiving feast, every person in our family was invited to mention one thing they were grateful for this past year. Four-year-old Tom couldn't remember anything, so he simply thanked God for "everything *next* year." Tom stretched us all to give deeper thanks since it is much easier to be grateful for past gifts than future gifts.

As Tom gave thanks for the future, so the Rite now calls on us to give praise to God for the future healing that will come through the anointing. If it seems strange to thank God for healing before we receive it, we should consider the words of Jesus, "I tell you therefore, everything you ask and pray for, believe that you have it already and it will be yours" (Mk 11:24). Our faith leads us to expect that Jesus will come as the Bread of Life at the Eucharist and we give praise and thanks before we receive him. We can also have as firm a belief leading us to praise and thank Jesus in advance for his expected, certain healing. A God who is more Mother and Father than the best human parents, Jesus who comes to live among us and heal us, the Holy Spirit our Consoler, are ready to do anything that is best for us if we prepare our hearts with praise and thanksgiving.

Praise itself can be very healing when it lifts us out of ourselves and into the presence of God. Whatever our burdens, they are easier to carry or they may even disappear when we pause to consider the magnitude of God's love for us.

Many charismatic prayer groups have discovered the importance of having an extended period of praise and thanksgiving at the beginning of the meeting in order to focus on the "goodness of God." Praise creates an atmosphere which allows us to become so receptive to Jesus' healing love that very little time needs to be spent on intercessory prayer.

During our workshops, we have noted an increase in the number of healings which occur when the participants are willing to spend extended time in thanksgiving prayer. Perhaps this is one of the reasons why St. James prefaced his teaching about anointing the sick by saying, "Is anyone cheerful? Let that person sing praise" (Jas 5:13).

—*Barbara*
—*Matt and Dennis*

Chapter 8
Anointing with Oil

Prayer heals not according to its length but according to its love, channeling Jesus' love and mercy given by his Spirit. The prayer that brought Lazarus back to life was simply one loving sentence, "Lord, he whom you love is sick" (Jn 11:4). Five-year-old Ricky continues to heal his family of flu, colds, backaches, with great childlike faith reminding Jesus, "Mommy's back hurts."

A first-grade teacher asks her pupils to pray for those who are absent and finds the first-graders' confident prayers produce major healings. Many prayer groups intercede for healing by simply praying with a heart full of the love of the Holy Spirit. The important thing is not the words or use of oil, but our desire to bless one another.

The oil should be applied as lovingly as Mary anointed Jesus' head at Bethany (Mk 14:3). Oil and this book's suggestions are merely a means for exercising spiritual help, and are useless instruments without the Holy Spirit's love in the user's heart.

We would expect a long, stately prayer to form the climax of the new Rite, but, instead, find that the priest prays only two sentences while anointing the sick person on the forehead and hands:

> Through this holy anointing may the Lord in his love and mercy help you with the grace of the Holy Spirit. May the Lord who freed you from sin save you and raise you up.[1]

This prayer forms a fitting climax because it briefly sums up the entire Rite. Since a priest prays the sacramental prayer in the name of the community, this prayer makes Jesus' love present in the entire community of the Church (introductory rite). It again reminds us of Jesus' "mercy" in freeing the sick from sin (penitential rite), and Jesus' mind and heart sent to "love" the sick (scripture reading).

Finally, "May the Lord who freed you from sin save you and raise you up" corresponds to the plea of the litany, while the anointing of the hands and forehead with oil brings both the healing power of touch and the healing power of oil in order to confer health of mind, body and soul.

When the Rite uses oil to ask for spiritual help, usually only the forehead and hands are anointed, although "the number of anointings is to be adapted to the occasion." Early Christians anointed any area of the body affected by illness. The eleventh century prayer of Theodulf advised a minimum of fifteen anointings, while the Council of Trent directed that the five senses be anointed for purification. The new Rite no longer emphasizes anointing and purifying the senses, but offers to the sick, Jesus' healing love and mercy through his Spirit. Though we don't anoint and purify the senses, we do find it helpful, when convenient, to anoint especially the part of the body in which the sickness or pain is centered.

Though the Rite allows for anointing various parts of the body, it stresses anointing the forehead and hands. The anointing of the forehead reminds us to ask the Spirit for peace of mind. Anointing the hands recalls that we are also praying for physical strength to flow out to the extremities so they can become Jesus' hands in loving service, embracing his cross redemptively until healing arrives. By the anointing we proclaim that the sick person is becoming *Christ* (meaning "the anointed one"), in the most loving way Jesus can come.

Oil is blessed and used, not just because Jesus sent out his Apostles to anoint (Mk 6:13), and because James says, "they must anoint the sick with oil," but because oil also symbolizes the way in which the Spirit is at work to heal the whole person—physically, mentally and spiritually.

Oil was used for physical healing in ancient times, e.g., the Good Samaritan poured oil into the wounds of the traveler to Jericho (Lk 10:34). Even today oil forms the base of most modern medicines, as well as the plastics used in surgical gloves and disposable syringes. The anointing with oil reminds us to pray over and use modern medicines; not to

throw away our pills to "claim a healing" unless the doctor
verifies the action. The book of Sirach reminds us of the
ancient wisdom, a wisdom even more true today with the
advances of medicine:

> My [child], when you are ill, do not be depressed,
> but pray to [God, who] will heal you. Renounce
> your faults, keep your hands unsoiled, and
> cleanse your heart from all sin. Offer incense and
> a memorial of fine flour, and make as rich an offer-
> ing as you can afford. Then let the doctor take
> over—[God] created [the doctor] too—and do
> not let [them] leave you, for you need [them].
> Sometimes success is in their hands, since they in
> turn will beseech the Lord to grant them the grace
> to relieve and to heal, that life may be saved. A
> [person] sins in the eyes of his [or her] Maker if he
> [or she] defies the doctor.
>
>   (Sir 38:9–15)

Sirach's words "to pray to the Lord. . . . and then let the
doctor take over" echo closely the plea of St. Caesarius of
Arles (c. 525 A.D.) who healed many through prayer and
anointing, yet continued to wish, "If at least they would
look for health from ordinary medical care."[2] But prayer
can also enrich "ordinary medical care" as it performs its
daily tasks such as diagnosing illness or prescribing medicine. For instance, cancer specialist and noted author, Dr.
Larry Samuels, finds that his days of highest accuracy with
his cancer scanner are those days when he prays for guidance before seeing each patient.[3]

Doctors, nurses and patients can pray not only for help

in the diagnosis, but also for Jesus to bless the medicine or surgery so it will heal faster. One nurse who prayed over her tray of medicine, reported that she needed to administer one-third the normal pain medication.

We can continue in the tradition of St. Basil who healed the sick both by prayer and by building the first hospital. Christianity differs from other world religions in its desire to bring God's healing through the medical profession.[4]

Oil calls us to expect physical healing as well as emotional healing of our fears, anger and guilt. The ancient Jewish law permitted anointings to occur during hopeful times of feasts, and to be omitted when a person desired to fast and mourn. (Cf. Ruth 3:3; Mt 6:17). Esteemed guests were anointed, while hidden anger made Simon the Pharisee neglect to anoint Jesus (Lk 7:46). The anointing with oil is a sign that we expect to be filled with hope and become one with those around us.

Oil calls us to be spiritually healed in order to become one with Jesus. It proclaims our identity with Jesus just as he prayed we would become one with him. We have been anointed with health and with the Spirit in order to use that health in Jesus' mission "to bring good news to the poor" (Is 61:1). We can expect what David experienced when anointed by Samuel, "From that day on the Spirit of the Lord rushed upon David" (1 Sam 16:13).

—Matt and Dennis

As the priest anoints the sick person with oil, he is bringing comfort to a suffering body and conferring new life to a spirit. Because the oil has been blessed to convey wholeness, it is more than a light-colored fluid; it is a powerful means for carrying God's healing love.

More than once I've observed dramatic changes in a person's condition immediately following the anointing with oil. For instance, a small child, who was experiencing constant convulsive seizures, became relaxed and peaceful as she was blessed with holy oil. Another time a truck driver bleeding profusely from a deep laceration of his forehead was almost instantaneously healed as a modern-day good Samaritan anointed him with oil while they were awaiting the arrival of an ambulance. The emergency room physician did not even need to suture the wound because it had nearly disappeared.

This portion of the rite of Anointing emphasizes the effectiveness of holy oil for the restoration of our entire being. Most of us, at some time in our lives, have experienced the beneficial effects of soothing oil. It is beautiful to observe the contented expression on the face of an infant as the mother gently massages sweet smelling liquid into the skin. Hospital patients consider it a special treat to receive a backrub accompanied by the application of an oil-base lotion. Most salves for itches, burns or scratches contain some form of oil reminding us of the universal use of this substance.

Matt and Dennis gave an example of a nurse who prayed over pain medication with interesting results. I would like to encourage everyone to pray over any type of medicine they are taking, asking Jesus to bless it and make it useful for healing. Most Christians would never partake of a meal without saying a blessing over the food, yet we fail to have the same consideration for the medicine we ingest. We can ask Jesus to remove any side effects from the drugs we take and infuse them with God's healing power. I know of several persons who were completely protected from the adverse effects of cancer chemotherapy and radiation through the power of prayer which surrounded them during their treatments. They were certainly following the injunction of St. Paul, "Whatever you eat, whatever you drink, whatever you do at all, do it for the glory of God" (1 Cor 10:31).

There is no conflict between medicine and healing prayer—both methods can work in partnership to bring wholeness to the individual. Our modern hospital system was founded by Christian women and men who recognized the necessity of treating the total person through every means available. In recent years there has been a renewal of spirituality among many members of the medical profession, prompting the formation of the Association of Christian Therapists in 1975.[5] This professional organization seeks to bring together all branches of medicine in order to explore the correlation between prayer and wholeness. There cannot be true healing unless the entire person is freely functioning in body, mind and spirit, a process which requires a lifetime of integration.

Many centuries ago, the philosopher Plato warned: "This is the great error of our day in the treatment of the human body, that physicians separate the soul from the body." In our modern scientific world we are just beginning to recognize the truth of that statement. Much evidence is being compiled in medical journals concerning psychosomatic illnesses (psyche-soul, soma-body), and the list grows longer every day. There is much we do not understand about the relationship between soul and body but, balancing the two is one of the purposes of this sacrament.

—***Barbara***

Chapter 9
Prayer after Anointing

Just as the sun has more warmth when focused to a pinpoint through a magnifying glass, so, too, the healing love of Jesus seems to intensify when focused through specific prayer. After the general prayer for healing, the priest must select one of the following:

1) full health with no pain;
2) health coming through suffering;
3) health and patience for coping with the weakness of old age;
4) strength and hope of salvation for those in great danger; and,
5) strength, forgiveness and relief of pain for those about to die.

The priest prays both for healing and for strength to endure the suffering so the illness can be redemptive and growthful until total healing comes. Too often we pray either for healing or for the sick to have strength "to bear their cross of sickness," when Jesus wants to enable us to do both in the process of healing. Thus the purpose of the rite is not only to help the sick person "to bear his suffering bravely, but also to fight against it."[1]

Jesus' healing can range from full health to the ultimate healing—healing of the body through death. How do we discern the way Jesus wants to heal this person? Rev. Tommy Tyson answers, "I give one ear to the sick person and the better ear to Jesus." Thus we listen to the sick person, listen to Jesus, and pray in the way the Holy Spirit leads. Some people seem to receive a "word from the Lord," or an image, helping them to focus their prayer on the specific way Jesus wants to work. However, Dennis notes that he finds it difficult to sort out Jesus' desires from his own human compassion.

"Rather than relying totally on my feelings, I find it helpful to simply ask the sick person after a few minutes of prayer, 'What are you experiencing' His answer helps me to discover how Jesus appears to be working.

"An elderly woman with back problems told me through tears that she had just lost her husband. I prayed then, not for the physical healing of her back, but for inner healing of her grief. As the grief was unloaded through tears, the love of Jesus poured into her heart and her back pain began to disappear."

Recently a woman with her arm in a sling asked for prayers. After a few minutes Matt asked what she was experiencing. "She felt a tingling and warmth in her toes, so I shifted from her arm to praying for her chronic hammer toes which rapidly began to spread out. Healing seems to occur more frequently when, after listening to the person, we ask Jesus how to pray, pray a while, and then discern further by simply asking the person what she is experiencing. In this way we are calling upon all the resources available to us as we try to discover the direction of our prayers."

—Matt and Dennis

The prayer after anointing instructs those praying to discern the most appropriate way to pray for the sick person. It is a reminder of the importance of seeking God's guidance when we intercede for others. Much energy can be expended petitioning Jesus for answers which may not be beneficial to ourselves or others. One way of overcoming this obstacle is to ask the question, "Jesus, how can I best pray for this person?"

When we ask Jesus how to best pray for another we are truly seeking their greatest potential. Sometimes this may seem logical to the mind but senseless to the heart if we begin to discern the person's life on earth is ending. Thus the time of prayer after the anointing can provide an opportunity for all who are in attendance to ask for courage to confront the outcome of the illness.

I was privileged to be at the bedside of a dear friend who had valiantly battled against bone cancer. As her body became ravaged by the illness, her spirit seemed to take on a sense of peace and tranquillity. She told me she had seen a vision of heaven and couldn't wait to get there. As her family gathered for the Rite of Anointing, they assured Pat that God wanted to physically heal her now. They exhorted her to have faith as they read selected scripture passages to her.

When it came time for the prayer after the anointing, I invited them to quietly listen as we asked Jesus to guide our prayer intention. Soon one of Pat's brothers began to weep as he softly said, "I think Jesus is here to take Pat home." At first the others seemed startled by this statement, then one by one they expressed similar feelings.

It was then Pat's turn to pray. She asked Jesus to comfort the hearts of her loved ones and give them peace regarding her condition. Several days later she quietly 'went home.' At the funeral service her family shared the story of that moment at her bedside. It was a tender moment that continued to bring them consolation in the midst of grief.

The Holy Spirit often guides us to pray for total wholeness in a person's life. Sometimes we receive scripture readings or prophetic words confirming that God wills to heal the sick one. If the person dies we can become confused over this apparent contradiction forgetting that eternal life does provide the ultimate healing. The book of Revelations describes the heavenly Jerusalem as a place where God will *"wipe away all tears from their eyes; there will be no more death, no more mourning or sadness, the world of the past has gone"* (Rev. 21:4, JB).

God alone can see the total picture of our lives and, as we seek wisdom, the path before us will illuminate the perfect way.

—**Barbara**

Chapter 10
The Lord's Prayer

We can be so familiar with the Our Father that we sometimes fail to pay attention to the meaning of this glorious prayer. The priest intones the first two words and we spontaneously recite the entire prayer.

The Lord's Prayer is placed in the Rite of Anointing not only as a preparation for Communion, but also to remind us that we are interceding for all God's sick children. We address God as a heavenly Father who desires wholeness for his sick child as much as a human mother or father does. "If you . . . know how to give your children what is good, how much more will your Father in heaven give good things to those who ask him!" (Mt 7:11). To the degree we direct God's love to the sick, we heal the sick. We ask that God's name be hallowed by the healing, just as Jesus asked for the blind to see so God might be glorified.

We are not asking just for health—but health which will enable us to be placed lovingly in God's service so the kingdom might come *now* upon the earth. When praying that God's will be done "on earth as it is in heaven," we are asking to receive at this moment the fullness of life. We are prone to use this portion of the prayer out of context when we stress the phrase, "your will be done," at the end of our prayers, without finishing the entire sentence. Expressing the whole thought places the emphasis on our expectancy that the heavenly kingdom, where there is no sickness, sorrow or death, will gradually come upon this earth.

For God's kingdom to come, we ask to receive strength through the direct touch of God's power and, also, through gifts of daily bread, including medicine, nutritious food and doctor's care. The Creator will use every means available in order to bring us into wholeness.

The burgeoning field of psychosomatic medicine reinforces the request to receive and give forgiveness of trespasses so we can be released from any anger or guilt which causes or prolongs our illness. Although we may not yet feel loving towards another, we can use our will to ask God to help us with resentment, hurt feelings or hatred. This act of the will opens the door of our spirit to enable God to begin to bless our lives.

The prayer finishes with a request to be protected from temptation and from all future evil leading to illness. This portion of the Our Father is actually a prayer for deliverance. All of us encounter evil every day, in such forms as oppression, injustice, racism, sexism, environmental pollution and broken relationships. Evil damages our bodies, minds and spirits. Whether this evil seems to us personal or impersonal, God wants to deliver us from it.

One temptation is to think healing is too complicated. Then we get discouraged before we begin. However, we needn't be confused by all the facets of the Rite of Anointing if we but recall the simplicity of the Lord's Prayer. It summarizes all that is necessary in approaching God, who is our loving Father and Mother.

—Barbara
—Matt and Dennis

Chapter 11
Communion

Communion is not just the act of becoming one with Jesus' Body in bread, but of becoming one with his body in people. We will be healthier to the degree that we see Jesus in the people who are continually hurting us. When the Eucharist becomes a commitment to love our enemy with the love of Jesus, then another level of healing begins. That's why St. Paul could tell the Corinthians who received the Eucharist, yet refused to share their food: "Everyone is to recollect himself before eating this bread and drinking this cup; because a person who eats and drinks without recognizing the Body is eating and drinking his own condemnation. In fact, that is why many of you are weak and ill and some of you have died" (1 Cor 11:28–30). The Eucharist's power to bring health increases when we receive not just bread but the whole Jesus present in his members.

Throughout history Christians have experienced health coming through the Eucharist. The earliest written rites, such as *Bishop Serapion's Prayer Book* (IV, 7) and the *Apostolic Constitutions* (VIII, 29) of Hippolytus, provide special prayers at the Eucharist for blessing oil, bread or even water to be used for healing the sick. St. Caesarius (502–542) also connects health with the Eucharist when he advises, "Come to Church, anoint yourselves with blessed oil, receive the Eucharist of Christ. If you do this, you will receive health not only for the body but also for the soul."[1]

Even today the oils for the Rite of Anointing the sick are blessed on Holy Thursday, the day dedicated to the institution of the Eucharist at the Last Supper. Each day the priest, before Communion, prays silently for "health of mind and body," then joins the people in praying the centurion's prayer for healing, "Lord, I am not worthy to receive you but only say the Word and I shall be healed." Healing is our last request before receiving the body and blood of Jesus.

The reports of healing through receiving the Body and Blood of Jesus in the Eucharist are as numerous as the pages of Christian history. The reports vary in their fact and fiction, but enough physical healing occurred that St. Caesarius (502–542 A.D.) and later St. Elygius (600 A.D.) were successful in having the sick reject their amulets and healing magic and receive the Eucharist and be anointed with oil.[2] Superstitious people switched from magic to the Eucharist, not because of a theology of Eucharistic healing, but because it worked! The earliest recorded rites for the sick, such as the Carolingian ritual, all include the Eucharist. If the sick were not healed immediately, prayers were to be repeated and the Eucharist to be received for seven days.

While working as hospital chaplains, we too saw the Eucharist physically heal in many dramatic ways, such as sudden positive changes recorded on heart monitors, rapid drops in temperature from 101.8 to 98.8, blood pressures spontaneously changing 20 points, and the most common—healing accelerated so a patient recovers and goes home in half the expected time.

As Catholics, we experience the Eucharist as a central source of healing. Those in nonsacramental churches may experience calling on the blood of Jesus as a central source of healing. But either one, can degenerate into a magical formula for healing. Healing happens to the degree we meet Jesus, give him thanks for whatever healing has begun, and rest in his love and power within us. We can invite Jesus to come within us (spiritual communion) and transform our body cell by cell into his body. Often it is helpful to imagine Jesus' healing power like light emanating from the Eucharist living within us and warming the area of the body that needs healing.

The word "Eucharist" means "give thanks." Gratitude opens our hearts and thereby helps us receive all the healing love that God wants to give us. Thus, when we lead a Eucharist for healing, we spend most of the time thanking Jesus for his gifts and past healing, and then finally intercede for present needs. Agnes Sanford, who was one of the most respected and wise teachers of healing prayer, emphasized strongly the need to finish healing prayer by giving thanks for healing that has already started.[4] The Eucharist heals not only by receiving Jesus in bread, but by also "giving thanks" for all he is accomplishing through this sacrament.

—Matt and Dennis

The celebration of Mass is a healing service, and the reception of Eucharist can be a powerful means for obtaining wholeness in body, mind and spirit. Jesus is present in the Eucharist in his resurrected person, filled with life and desiring to transfer this life into us. If we believe in this truth, we will be the healthiest of people.

Jesus told us, "whoever eats me will draw life from me" (Jn 6:57), as he encouraged us to receive his Body in order to become complete. As we approach the altar for Communion, it is helpful to consider any specific areas within us which need healing, and appropriate the power of Jesus to touch our needs. As far as we know, Jesus was never physically ill, nor did he suffer from emotional problems. Therefore, when we accept his Body into ours, we can expect greater wholeness.

The woman with a hemorrhage (Mt 9:20) understood this principle when she reached out her hand saying, "If I can only touch his cloak, I shall be well again." Her trust in Jesus' ability to cure her affliction brought new life into her body.

When we receive Jesus in the Eucharist, we are in even more intimate contact with the divine presence than this suffering woman. We are being permitted to partake of the total risen nature of Jesus, not with our fingertips but our whole being. The healer abides within us in a magnificent way, bringing light into the darkness of physical, emotional or spiritual wounds.

During one of our workshops for nurses, Mary O'Keefe from Baldwin, New York, shared this story:

> "Nine years ago I was diagnosed as having acute rheumatoid arthritis and was placed on cortisone and arthritis medication. During the next seven years, I experienced varying degrees of swelling, pain, discomfort and deformity in several different areas of my body. I was never able to be without some type of medication.
>
> "Two years ago I attended a Mass emphasizing 'Healing through the Eucharist.' Even though I had been involved in the Charismatic Renewal for one year, I had been afraid to ask for healing of my arthritis. That evening I *did* ask Jesus to heal me as I received him in Communion. Within a few weeks I noticed that my symptoms had disappeared, I was able to discontinue all medication and have had no recurrence.
>
> "Now I receive the Eucharist in thanksgiving for my continued good health."

This example is one of hundreds I have heard from Christians who seriously consider the reality of God's healing love through the reception of Holy Communion. We can similarly call upon this grace to assist us with emotional difficulties, remembering that the mind of Jesus is also resident in the sacrament.

A young friend of mine was in great need of inner healing for memories from his early childhood. His parents were killed in an airplane crash and he had been sent to live with various relatives, some of whom treated him cruelly. He asked me to pray with him but there always seemed to be last minute conflicts blocking our meeting.

One morning, while he was at Mass, he suddenly realized that Jesus, present in the Eucharist, was perfectly able to touch his unconscious mind and relieve him of the burdens he carried. As he received the Eucharist, he asked Jesus to go back into his childhood and free the little boy who felt so rejected and alone. In his imagination he pictured Jesus holding the child in his strong arms to protect him from harm. He experienced years of fear and tension being washed away as he thanked Jesus for giving him new life. This same life is readily available to all of us, each time we celebrate the Eucharist. The Rite of Anointing makes this healing power of the Eucharist available to the sick person.

—Barbara

Chapter 12
Blessing

The rite of the sick closes with one of two blessings for continued healing and protection from harm. The blessing asks that God's help may continue beyond our healing prayer together. Most healings are not immediate, but, rather, "process" healings that begin or continue days after the healing prayer. Even Jesus did not heal a certain blind man immediately, but had to pray again that the "walking trees" he saw would be focused into people (Mk 8:22–25).

The oldest written healing rite, Alcuin's Carolingian Order, advises that the entire rite be repeated daily for seven days.[1] Today's rite for the sick also advises that the ritual be repeated "if the sick person recovers after anointing, or if during the same illness the danger becomes more serious."[2] Since a person always gets at least a little better or worse, repeating the sacrament's healing prayer is encouraged.

Today we are beginning to see the wisdom of repeating the healing prayer. Francis MacNutt, with his extraordinary gift of praying for physical healing, claims that only 25% seem to be healed immediately, another 50% are healed gradually if they continue to pray for healing, and 25% seem not to be physically healed. Most are healed gradually if prayer is continued over days and months.

Unfortunately, this wisdom of continual prayer for healing is not as widely known as the practice of telling the sick to "claim their healing." We even saw a group try to get a man with a broken leg to walk on his leg and claim that it was healed. That might be valid if he is in the 25% that are immediately healed but, should he be among the other 75%, he could sustain a compound fracture. Somehow people feel that if they claim their healing, they are showing more faith and more will be done. Actually, it takes more faith to claim only as much as God has really healed, believe that God's way and time are more loving than our desires, and then to pray daily for further healing. Claiming healing that hasn't happened can ultimately undermine the person's faith in healing prayer, hurt her as she avoids the doctors and medication she needs, or prevent her from continuing soaking prayer that might bring greater wholeness. It's best to claim only what Jesus has done and what the doctor verifies.

As a general rule, the more serious and chronic the illness, the longer it takes continued soaking prayer for healing. What takes longer for medicine to heal generally takes longer for healing prayer, perhaps because prayer most often accelerates the natural process of healing. Accidental cuts usually need less prayer than chronic rheumatoid arthritis.

A close friend has been praying for several months with a woman who has an immobilized hand half its regular size. With weekly soaking prayer, sensation returned, then movement, then the fingers straightened slowly and the hand started to fill out. None of this would have happened if she had just prayed once. If something begins to happen, such as release from pain, it's usually a sign that Jesus will do more healing through soaking prayer.

Perhaps healing prayer by now sounds too complicated. It is as easy and as complex as loving. Lovers will daily find new ways to express their feelings for one another. Likewise, if we love the sick with Jesus' love, we will be led to pray in many ways not mentioned in this book. Healing the sick means prayerfully loving the sick as Jesus does. One mother who understands Jesus' heart and prays powerfully for healing revealed her secret: I love; I listen; I hug; I pray.

—Matt and Dennis

The Rite of Anointing concludes with a blessing by the priest which reads, in part: "May God the Father bless you;

may God the Son heal you; may God the Holy Spirit enlighten you."

We are invoking the Trinity and enlisting all assistance in the completion of our prayer for healing, as we thank God for things already accomplished and offer praise for what is still to come.

Matt and Dennis have already discussed the fact that healing is a process requiring us to continue seeking wholeness through all the means available to us. Many times we have witnessed spontaneous healings, sometimes of serious, chronic ailments, and it has filled our hearts with joy to see these manifestations of God's power.

However, we have not been oblivious to the sufferings of those who are not immediately set free. Kathryn Kuhlman summed it up when she said: "The first question I will ask Jesus when I get to heaven is, 'Why weren't they all healed?'" She has undoubtedly received the answer since she is no longer on earth while we must still walk by faith through the mysterious ways of God.

Although I don't know why everyone isn't healed, I do know we have been commanded to seek the wholeness which will help us to approach God and our neighbors in an ever deepening commitment of love. Anything which impedes the ability to love and be loved, is not in the will of God. If my physical condition is causing me to become so self-centered that I can no longer lovingly care for my family, it needs to be healed. If my mind is so confused I am no longer able to make rational decisions, I can be very certain that Jesus wants to set me free.

The problem arises when we attempt to make God into

our image and likeness instead of vice versa. God's time-
table for answered prayer may not be in accordance with
ours and, therefore, we may feel rejected and angry when
things don't live up to our expectations. However, if we
could see the situation with the eyes of Jesus, we would
realize the complexity of the entire process.

Jesus is not only healing our physical symptoms, but
also transforming the old thought patterns and bad habits
which caused us to be sick in the first place. Even those
who have been spontaneously freed from serious illnesses
usually are led through a period of spiritual renewal where
they are confronted with any disorder in their lives.

Jesus wants to bring abundant life to every portion of
our being. If we can patiently trust in his infinite goodness
as we ask for his healing love to become manifested, we
can keep ourselves from unhealthy anxiety and stress.

—Barbara

Epilogue
Prayer for Healing

The Rite of Anointing presents us with a means of experiencing the compassion and love of God. The steps in the sacrament are meant to lead us into an ever deepening awareness of God in our lives as we turn to the source of all life. God is not an abstract Deity but a Creator who desires to be intimately involved in every aspect of our search for wholeness.

God patiently waits to be invited into this process, since God never disregards our free will, but gives us the freedom to accept or reject the graces provided for us. Therefore, the first requirement for receiving Jesus' healing love is to place under God's dominion our entire being. We need to recognize our futile attempts to earn salvation through self-effort and receive the gift of unconditional love that Jesus gave us on the cross.

Perhaps you have a longing to invite Jesus more deeply into your life. He is already aware of your needs and is also longing to draw you closer to himself.

> Loving God, I realize there are many areas in my life where I need your healing touch. I have hesitated to ask for healing, but I come before you today, feeling somewhat like one half-dead on an abandoned roadside. I ask you to send Jesus down that roadway to care for me (Lk 10:29–37).
>
> Jesus, you come upon me with my bruises and open wounds. As you stop, your gaze sees all the events that caused those wounds and made me feel half-dead. As I feel your hand touching and examining each wound, I thank you that you are not like the priest and Levite, but that you love me just the way I am.
>
> Your healing touch invites me to open my squinting eyes. I feel your warm healing light penetrating through my eyes, filling my entire self, and infusing me with new life. Wherever I've been filled with darkness and despair, let your light penetrate those areas until I see through your eyes. (Pause and bask in Jesus' healing light.)
>
> As your interior warmth allows my whole body to become like wax ready to be reshaped, I give you all those parts of my body which have suffered from illness, especially any area that is in pain. Jesus, you know what it is like to endure pain; please anoint my body with your soothing oil, quiet the nerve endings and allow me to rest in comfort.

As I begin to rest in comfort, let me focus my attention on one physically wounded part of my body. Let me allow you to be the Good Samaritan as I feel the soothing of your oil and the gentleness of your bandage. Let me see how you reshape and restore that part of my body, just as you fashioned me with such exacting precision at the moment of my conception. (Pause and watch Jesus making your body new in the most loving way.)

And Jesus, when you were the good Samaritan, you made provisions with the innkeeper to continue the medical care and healing you had started. Bless those also who care for me when I am ill. Please give your gift of wisdom to my physician that he or she may be guided by your Holy Spirit. Bless too my medication and my nurses so that their hands will become your hands as they touch me.

Most of all, I ask you to fill my heart with your peace and love as a sure sign of your presence in me. As your presence touches my body and spirit in the most loving way, may we become more intimate so that at my death we will greet each other as old friends rather than as new acquaintances.

Sometimes we will be too weak or tired to pray like this. At such times healing prayer may be simply looking at a crucifix and repeating "Father, into your hands I commend my spirit" (Lk 23:46), as Jesus did long ago upon his cross on Calvary and as Jesus longs to do now upon his cross within us. Perhaps we want to rest in the arms of God the Mother, "like a child quieted at its mother's breast"

(Ps 131:2). We don't even need words, but can simply breathe in God's love and strength and breathe out the tension and discouragement, until our body feels relaxed and surrendered part by part. We can start with the wrinkles in the forehead and with each inhalation fill the forehead with God's love, and with each exhalation drain out the tension until the forehead feels relaxed and its cares are surrendered into God's hands. We can continue this meditation part by part down the eyes, face, jaw, neck and throughout the body until reaching the toes and wiggling them as does a child fondled by a parent's loving hand. We have a God who wants to heal us much more than any mother or father wants their child healed.

> Is there anyone among you who would hand his son a stone when he asked for bread? Or would hand him a snake when he asked for a fish? If you, then . . . know how to give your children what is good, how much more will your Father in heaven give good things to those who ask him! (Mt 7:9–11).

—Barbara
—Matt and Dennis

Appendices
Rite of Anointing a Sick Person

1. INTRODUCTORY RITE

Wearing the appropriate vestments, the priest approaches the sick person and greets him (her) and the others present in a friendly manner. He may use this greeting:

The peace of the Lord be with you.

According to the circumstances, the priest may sprinkle the sick person and the room with holy water, saying the following words or those given in a particular ritual:

**Let this water call to mind
your baptismal sharing
in Christ's redeeming passion and resurrection.**

95

Then he addresses those present in these or similar words:

> **Dear brothers and sisters,**
> **we have come together in the name of our Lord**
> **Jesus Christ, who restored the sick to health, and**
> **who himself suffered so much for our sake. He is**
> **present among us as we recall the words of the**
> **Apostle James: "Is there anyone sick among you?**
> **Let him call for the elders of the Church, and let**
> **them pray over him and anoint him in the name of**
> **the Lord. This prayer, made in faith, will save the**
> **sick man. The Lord will restore his health, and if he**
> **has committed any sins, they will be forgiven."**
> **Let us entrust our sick brother (sister) N. To the**
> **grace and power of Jesus Christ, that the Lord may**
> **ease his (her) suffering and grant him (her) health**
> **and salvation.**

2. PENITENTIAL RITE

If there is no sacramental confession, the penitential rite then follows.

> **My brothers and sisters, to prepare ourselves for this**
> **holy anointing, let us call to mind our sins.**

After a brief silence, all say:

> **I confess to almighty God,**
> **and to you, my brothers and sisters,**
> **that I have sinned through my own fault**
> **in my thoughts and in my words,**
> **in what I have done,**
> **and in what I have failed to do;**
> **and I ask blessed Mary, ever Virgin,**
> **all the angels and saints,**

> **and you, my brothers and sisters,**
> **to pray for me to the Lord our God.**

The priest concludes:

> **May almighty God have mercy on us,**
> **forgive us our sins,**
> **and bring us to everlasting life.**
> R. Amen.

3. READING FROM SCRIPTURE

Then a brief text from scripture is read by one of those present or by the priest.

> **Brothers and sisters, listen to the words of the Gospel according to John.**
>
> **Truly, truly, I say to you, he who believes in me will also do the works that I do: and greater works than these will he do, because I go to the Father. Whatever you ask in my name, I will do it, that the Father may be glorified in the Son. If you ask anything in my name, I will do it (Jn 14:12−14).**

4. LITANY

> **My brothers and sisters, with faith let us ask the Lord to hear our prayers for our brother (sister) N.**
>
> **Lord, through this holy anointing, come and comfort N. With your love and mercy.**
> R. Lord, hear our prayer.
> **Free N. From all harm.**
> R. Lord, hear our prayer.
> **Relieve the suffering of all the sick (here present).**

R. Lord, hear our prayer.
Assist all those dedicated to the care of the sick.
R. Lord, hear our prayer.
Free N. from sin and all temptation.
R. Lord, hear our prayer.
Give life and health to our brother (sister) N., on whom we lay our hands in your name.
R. Lord, hear our prayer.

5. LAYING ON OF HANDS

The priest then lays his hands on the head of the sick person in silence.

6. BLESSING OF OIL

**Let us pray.
Lord God, loving Father,
you bring healing to the sick
through your Son Jesus Christ.
Hear us as we pray to you in faith,
and send the Holy Spirit, man's Helper and Friend,
upon this oil, which nature has provided
to serve the needs of men.
May your blessing +
come upon all who are anointed with this oil,
that they may be freed from pain and illness
and made well again in body, mind and soul.
Father, may this oil be blessed for our use
in the name of our Lord Jesus Christ
who lives and reigns with you for ever and ever.**
R. Amen.

7. PRAYER OF THANKSGIVING

If the oil is already blessed, the priest says the prayer of thanksgiving over it:

> **Praise to you, almighty God and Father.**
> **You sent your Son to live among us and bring us salvation.**
> R. Blessed be God.
> **Praise to you, Lord, Jesus Christ,**
> **the Father's only Son.**
> **You humbled yourself to share in our humanity,**
> **and you desired to cure all our illnesses.**
> R. Blessed be God.
> **Praise to you, God the Holy Spirit, the Consoler.**
> **You heal our sickness with your mighty power.**
> R. Blessed be God.
> **Lord God,**
> **with faith in you**
> **our brother (sister)**
> **will be anointed with this holy oil.**
> **Ease his (her) sufferings and strengthen him (her) in his (her) weakness.**
> **We ask this through Christ our Lord.**
> R. Amen.

8. ANOINTING

Then the priest takes the oil and anoints the sick person on the forehead and the hands, saying once:

> **Through this holy anointing**
> **may the Lord in his love and mercy help you**
> **with the grace of the Holy Spirit.**
> R. Amen.

9. PRAYER AFTER ANOINTING

Afterwards the priest says one of the following prayers:

Let us pray.

A) *For full health with no pain*

> **Lord Jesus Christ, our Redeemer,**
> **by the power of the Holy Spirit**
> **ease the sufferings of our sick brother (sister)**
> **and make him (her) well again in mind and body.**
> **In your loving kindness forgive his (her) sins**
> **and grant him (her) full health**
> **so that he (she) may be restored to your service.**
> **You are Lord for ever and ever.**
> R. Amen.

B) *For health coming through suffering*

> **Lord Jesus Christ,**
> **you shared in our human nature**
> **to heal the sick and save all mankind.**
> **Mercifully listen to our prayers**
> **for the physical and spiritual health of our sick**
>   **brother (sister)**
> **whom we have anointed in your name.**
> **May your protection console him (her)**
> **and your strength make him (her) well again.**
> **[Help him (her) find hope in suffering,**
> **for you have given him (her) a share in your**
>   **passion.]**
> **You are Lord for ever and ever.**
> R. Amen.

C) *When the illness is the result of advanced age*

> **Lord,**
> **look kindly on our brother (sister)**
> **who has grown weak under the burden of his (her)**
> **years.**
> **In this holy anointing**
> **he (she) asks for the grace of health in body and**
> **soul.**
> **By the power of your Holy Spirit,**
> **make him (her) firm in faith and sure in hope,**
> **so that his (her) cheerful patience**
> **may reveal your love for us.**
> **We ask this through Christ our Lord.**
> R. Amen.

D) *When the sick person is in great danger*

> **Lord Jesus Christ,**
> **you took our weakness on yourself**
> **and bore our sufferings in your passion and death.**
> **Hear this prayer for our suffering brother (sister) N.**
> **You are his (her) redeemer:**
> **strengthen his (her) hope for salvation**
> **and in your kindness sustain him (her)**
> **in body and soul.**
> **You live and reign for ever and ever.**
> R. Amen.

E) *For those about to die*

> **Lord God, loving Father,**
> **you are the source of all goodness and love,**

and you never refuse forgiveness
to those who are sorry for their sins.
Have mercy on your son (daughter) N.,
who is about to return to you.
May this holy anointing
and our prayers made in faith assist him (her):
relieve his (her) pain, in body and soul,
forgive all his (her) sins,
and strengthen him (her) with your loving
    protection.
We ask this, Father, through your Son Jesus Christ,
who conquered death
and opened for us the way to eternal life,
and who lives and reigns for ever and ever.

R. Amen.

10. LORD'S PRAYER

Now let us pray to God as our Lord Jesus Christ
    taught us.
All: Our Father, . . .

11. COMMUNION

This is the Lamb of God
who takes away the sins of the world.
Happy are those who are called to his supper.
R. Lord, I am not worthy to receive you,
but only say the word and I shall be healed.
The body of Christ (or: the blood of Christ.)

R. Amen.

After a period of silence, the priest concludes with:

Let us pray.
God our Father, almighty and eternal,
we confidently call upon you,
that the body (and blood) of Christ
which our brother (sister) has received
may bring him (her)
lasting health in mind and body.
We ask this through Christ our Lord.
R. Amen.

12. BLESSING

May God the Father bless you.
R. Amen.
May God the Son heal you.
R. Amen.
May God the Holy Spirit enlighten you.
R. Amen.
May God protect you from harm
and grant you salvation.
R. Amen.
May he shine on your heart
and lead you to eternal life.
R. Amen.
[And may almighty God,
the Father, and the Son, + and the Holy Spirit,
bless you all.]
R. Amen.

Blessing of Oil,
For Use By Laity.*

Our help is in the name of the Lord,
R. Who made heaven and earth.

EXORCISM

God's creature, oil,
I cast out the demon from you by God the Father
    almighty +
who made heaven and earth and sea and all
that they contain.
Let the adversary's power, the devil's legions,
and all Satan's attacks and machinations
be dispelled and driven afar from this creature, oil.
Let it bring health in body and mind to all who use
    it,
in the name of God + the Father almighty,
and of our Lord Jesus Christ + his Son,
and of the Holy Spirit + the Advocate,
as well as in the love of the same Jesus Christ our
    Lord,
who is coming to judge both the living and the dead
and the world by fire.
R. Amen.
Lord, heed my prayer.
R. And let my cry be heard by you.

---

*The Roman Ritual, transl. by Philip Weller (Milwaukee: Bruce, 1964). p. 573.

The Lord be with you.
R. And also with you.

Let us pray.
Lord God almighty, before whom the hosts of angels
stand in awe
and whose heavenly service we acknowledge,
may it please you to regard favorably
and to bless and hallow this creature, oil,
which by your power has been pressed from the
juice of olives.
You have ordained it for anointing the sick, so that,
when they are made well, they may give thanks to
you,
the living and true God.
Grant, we pray, that those who use this oil,
which we are blessing + in your name,
may be delivered from all suffering, all infirmity,
and all wiles of the enemy.
Let it be a means of averting any kind of adversity
from man,
made in your image and redeemed by the precious
blood of your son,
so that he may never again suffer the sting of the
ancient serpent,
through Christ our Lord.
R. Amen.

The oil is sprinkled with holy water.

For more on the lay use of blessed oil, see "A Lay Person Can Anoint Licitly with Blessed Oil," *Homiletic & Pastoral Review* (January, 1982) pp. 67–68.

Footnotes

Foreword to the Revised Edition

1. Claudia Wallis, "Faith & Healing: Can Spirituality Promote Health?", *Time* (June 24, 1996), pp. 58–64.

2. Larry Dossey, M.D., *Healing Words: The Power of Prayer and the Practice of Medicine* (New York: Harper Collins, 1992), pp. 251–253.

3. Dossey, *op. cit.*, p. 180.

4. *Idem.*

Introduction

1. Barbara Shlemon, *Healing Prayer* (Notre Dame: Ave Maria Press, 1976).

Prologue

1. Much of the historical material in this book comes from a doctoral dissertation "Relationship Between the Sacrament of Anointing the Sick and the Charism of Healing Within the Catholic Charismatic Renewal." Louis Rogge, O.Carm., is currently writing this dissertation for Union Theological Seminary. Unless otherwise indicated, the historical material for this text comes from Louis Rogge and four other sources: 1. Morton Kelsey, *Healing and Christianity* (New York: Harper & Row, 1973). 2. Placid Murray, O.S.B., "The Liturgical History of Extreme Unction," in *The Furrow*, XI (1960), 572–593, citing Antoine Chavasse, *Etude*

II (unpublished). 3. Paul F. Palmer, S.J., ed., *Sacraments and Forgiveness: History and Doctrinal Development of Penance, Extreme Unction and Indulgences,* Vol 2 of *Source of Christian Theology* (Westminster, Maryland: The Newman Press, 1959). 4. Bernhard Poschmann, S.J., *Penance and Anointing of the Sick,* tr. Francis Courteney (N.Y.: Herder, 1964).

Chapter 1

1. Henry James Coleridge, *Life and Letters of Francis Xavier* (London: Burns & Oates, 1874), 154–155.

2. Innocent I, *Epistolae et Decreta* 25,8.

3. Louis P. Rogge, O.Carm., "The Anointing of the Sick in Historical Perspective," *Linacre Quarterly,* 42:3 (August, 1975), 205–214.

4. Paul F. Palmer, S.J. "Who Can Anoint the Sick?" *Worship* 48:2 (February, 1974), 84–85.

5. *Rite of Anointing and Pastoral Care of the Sick* (N.Y.: Pueblo, 1974), 26. Will be referred to as *Rite of Anointing.*

6. *Ibid.,* 23.

7. *Ibid.,* 26.

8. *Ibid.,* 51.

9. Bishops' Committee on the Liturgy, *Study Text II: Anointing and Pastoral Care of the Sick: Commentary on the Rite for the Anointing and Pastoral Care of the Sick* (Washington: United States Catholic Conference, 1973), 22.

10. *Rite of Anointing,* 16.

11. Francis MacNutt, *The Power to Heal* (Notre Dame: Ave Maria Press, 1977), 47. Besides this book, Francis MacNutt's book, *Healing* (Notre Dame: Ave Maria Press, 1974) gives valuable information about why and how to pray for physical healing.

Chapter 2

1. *Rite of Anointing,* 50.

2. For a treatment of sacramental confession as healing see Michael Scanlan, T.O.R., *The Power in Penance* (Notre Dame: Ave Maria Press, 1972).

3. W.B. Cannon, "The Emergency Functions of the Adrenal Medulla in Pain and Major Emotions," *American Journal of Physiology,* 33 (1914), 356.

4. Meyer Friedman and Ray Rosenman, *Type-A Behavior and Your Heart* (Greenwich, CT: Fawcett, 1974).

5. For the relationship of emotional and physical components of var-

ious illnesses, see: David Graham, "Psychosomatic Medicine," in *Handbook of Psychophysiology,* ed. By Greenfield, Norman, and Sternbach (N.Y.: Holt, Rinehart and Winston, 1972), 839–924.

6. Hans Selye, *the Stress of Life* (N.Y.: McGraw-Hill, 1956).

Chapter 3

1. For a basic treatment of healing through active imagination, cf. Ruth Stapleton, *The Gift of Inner Healing* (Waco, Texas: Word, 1976) and *the Experience of Inner Healing* (Waco, Texas: Word, 1977). Also cf. Morton Kelsey, *the Other Side of Silence* (N.Y.: Paulist, 1976) for the importance of imagination in prayer.

2. O. Carl Simonton and Stephanie S. Simonton, "Belief Systems and Management of Malignancy," *Journal of Transpersonal Psychology,* VII:1 (1975), 29–47.

Chapter 4

1. A study by biologist Bernard Grad of MiGill University in Montreal has demonstrated the efficacy of prayer when people who are sick themselves pray for other sick people. Cited in Bernie Siegel, *Peace, Love & Healing* (New York: Harper, 1989), 253.

Chapter 5

1. Irenaeus, *Contra Haeresis* II:32,4–5.

2. Ronald Sullivan, "Hospitals Introducing a Therapy Resembling 'Laying On of Hands,'" *New York Times* (New York: Nov 6, 1977).

3. Godfrey Diekmann, O.S.B., "The Laying on of Hands: The Basic Sacramental Rite," The Catholic Theological Society of America, *Proceedings of the Twenty-Ninth Annual Convention* (Chicago: 1974), 340.

Chapter 6

1. Probably A.D. 197; cf. Cyril Richardson, "The Date and Setting of the Apostolic Tradition of Hippolytus: A Preliminary Essay," *Anglican Theological Review* 30 (1948), 39,41.

2. Matthew and Dennis Linn, *Healing of Memories* (N.Y.: Paulist, 1974); idem, *Healing Life's Hurts* (N.Y.: Paulist, 1978). For a treatment of emotional healing through prayer.

3. Francis MacNutt, *Power to Heal, op.cit.,* 247–48.

Chapter 8

1. *Rite of Anointing and Pastoral Care of the Sick,* (N.Y.: Catholic Book Publishing Co., 1974), 66–67.

2. Caesarius, *Sermo* 52,5.

3. We are indebted to our friend Larry Samuels, M.D., author of *Cancer Diagnosis in Children* (Cleveland: C.R.C. Press, 1972), for not only teaching us the importance of prayer for guidance, but also for helping us understand the relationship between emotions and illnesses such as cancer.

4. Hans Kung, *On Being a Christian* (Garden City, N.Y.: Doubleday, 1976), 577.

5. Further information can be obtained by writing: Assn. Of Christian Therapists, 6728 Old McLean Village Dr., McLean VA 22101, (703) 556-9222.

Chapter 9

1. *Rite of Anointing,* 15.

Chapter 11

1. Placid Murray, O.S.B., "The Liturgical History of Extreme Unction," *The Furrow,* XI (1960), 578.

2. Eligius, *De rectitudine catholicae conversationis,* 5.

3. James Brassil, *And I Will Fill This House With Glory: Renewal Within a Suburban Parish* (Locust Valley, N.Y.: Living Flame Press, 1977).

4. Agnes Sanford, *The Healing Light* (Plainfield, N.J.: Logos, 1947).

Chapter 12

1. Boone Porter, "The Origin of the Medieval Rite for Anointing the Sick or Dying," *The Journal of Theological Studies* New Series 7:2 (October, 1956), 214–223.

2. *Rite of Anointing,* 16.

Resources for Further Growth by the Authors

Dennis and Matthew Linn (and Sheila Fabricant Linn).

In follow-up to this book we especially recommend *Healing of Memories* (1974), *Healing Life's Hurts* (1978; revised 1993), *Praying with Another for Healing* (1984), *Healing the Eight Stages of Life* (1988), *Good Goats: Healing our Image of God* (1994) and *Simple Ways to Pray for Healing* (1998), all published by Paulist Press.

For further information about these books, as well as other books and tapes by the authors, please contact:

Christian Video Library
3914-A Michigan Avenue
St. Louis, MO 63118
Phone (314) 865-0729, FAX (314) 773-3115

For information about retreats and conferences with the Linns, please contact them in care of Re-Member Ministries at the above address, phone (970) 476-9235 or (314) 865-0729, FAX (970) 476-9235 or (314) 773-3115.

Barbara Shlemon Ryan

In follow-up to this book I especially recommend two of my other books: *Healing Prayer* (1974), and *Healing the Hidden Self* (1982) both published by Ave Maria Press, Notre Dame, IN 46556, 1-800-282-1865.

In 1977, the administrator at St. Vincent Hospital and Medical Center in Toledo, Ohio, agreed to permit a group of Christians to pray with a number of hospitalized patients. The medical staff was available to determine the effectiveness of those prayers using blood tests, x-rays and other diagnostic tools.

The prayer team was headed by Francis MacNutt and included Barbara Shlemon, RN, Sr. Jeanne Hill, O.P., and Fr. Paul Schaaf. Twenty of the 24 patients demonstrated significant clinical changes during the two day period. A 28 minute video of this event, containing teachings on how to pray for the sick is available from:

Beloved Ministry
PO Box 9249
Brea, CA, 92822
Phone 714-671-5835
Fax 714-671-3041

For information about retreats and conferences given by Barbara, please contact Timothy Ryan at Beloved Ministry.

Published by Resurrection Press

A Rachel Rosary *Larry Kupferman*	$3.95
Catholic Is Wonderful *Mitch Finley*	$4.95
Common Bushes *Kieran Kay*	$8.95
Christian Marriage *John & Therese Boucher*	$3.95
From Holy Hour to Happy Hour *Francis X. Gaeta*	$7.95
The Gift of the Dove *Joan M. Jones, PCPA*	$3.95
Healing through the Mass *Robert DeGrandis, SSJ*	$7.95
Healing the Wounds of Emotional Abuse *Nancy Benvenga*	$6.95
Healing Your Grief *Ruthann Williams, OP*	$7.95
Let's Talk *James P. Lisante*	$7.95
A Celebration of Life *Anthony Padovano*	$7.95
Heart Business *Dolores Torrell*	$6.95
A Path to Hope *John Dillon*	$6.95
Inwords *Mary Kraemer, OSF*	$4.50
The Healing of the Religious Life *Faricy/Blackborow*	$6.95
The Joy of Being a Catechist *Gloria Durka*	$4.50
Transformed by Love *Margaret Magdalen, CSMV*	$5.95
RVC Liturgical Series: The Liturgy of the Hours	$3.95
The Lector's Ministry	$3.95
Loving Yourself for God's Sake *Adolfo Quezada*	$5.95
Young People and . . . You Know What *William O'Malley*	$3.50
Lights in the Darkness *Ave Clark, O.P.*	$8.95
Practicing the Prayer of Presence *van Kaam/Muto*	$7.95
5-Minute Miracles *Linda Schubert*	$3.95
Stress and the Search for Happiness *van Kaam/Muto*	$3.95
Harnessing Stress *van Kaam/Muto*	$3.95
Healthy and Holy under Stress *van Kaam/Muto*	$3.95
Season of New Beginnings *Mitch Finley*	$4.50
Season of Promises *Mitch Finley*	$4.50
Soup Pot *Ethel Pochocki*	$8.95
Stay with Us *John Mullin, SJ*	$3.95
Still Riding the Wind *George Montague*	$7.95
Surprising Mary *Mitch Finley*	$7.95

Resurrection Press books and cassettes are available in your local religious bookstore. If you want to be on our mailing list for our up-to-date announcements, please write or phone:

Resurrection Press, P.O. Box 248, Williston Park, NY 11596
1-800-89 BOOKS